Foldy Rolly Patchwork Pzzazz

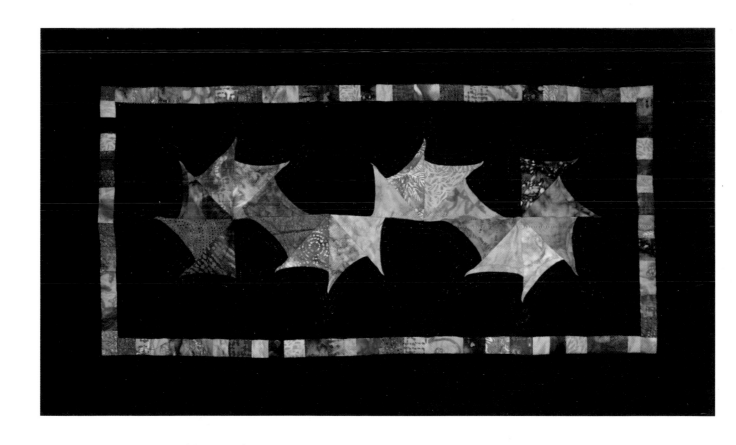

Jennie Rayment

Acknowledgements

This book is dedicated to my husbands, not only to those passed and present, but especially to the latest and most forbearing one, Nick Diment. He tolerates tantrums, tears and distress, jollies me along and administers a good kick (metaphorically) when necessary, and has once more proof read all the text for this seventh book. He must be mad!

I am very grateful to Patsy Yardley for volunteering to check the proofs yet again. She has worked extremely hard correcting my various mistakes and as expected proffered some invaluable advice. Many thanks are also extended to Lynn Manley for reading thoroughly, discovering and correcting some howlers and offering her technical expertise. Florien de Walle, my daughter-in-law, gets my enduring gratitude as she not only read the text, proffered many sensible suggestions and despite not being a stitcher managed to make up the designs whilst looking after young William. He at the tender age of 10 months was press ganged into modelling the Quag!

In addition, I extend my appreciation and thanks to Ann Seed, Lin Barratt, Lindsey Smith and Ngaire Lang who made quilts using the block designs, all four girls were taught most capably by Jeanne Stetson. Shelagh Jarvis has come up trumps again and turned her needle skills and artistic ability to good use and created several articles for this book. Eva Bishop took some amazingly creative photographs that are used within the text and also produced the final design for the front cover.

Finally, a big thank you to all my students who still continue to support me and indeed still obey (sometimes) my commands, even if I have to peer over the top of my glasses to quell any unruly bod who dares to query my words of wisdom.

If I have omitted to say a thank you to anyone else - please accept my apologies, put it down to too much twiddling and fiddling and a brain filled with fluff and threads!

Copyright © Jennie Rayment 2011
First Published August 2011

ISBN - 13: 978-0-9524675-9-5
ISBN - 10: 0-9524675-9-3

J. R. Publications
5 Queen Street, Emsworth,
Hampshire, PO10 7BJ. England
Tel/Fax: +44 (0)1243 374860
e-mail: jenrayment@aol.com
web site: www.jennierayment.com

Printed by Holbrooks Printers Ltd
Norway Road, Hilsea
Portsmouth, Hampshire PO3 5HX. England
Tel: 02392 661485 Fax: 02392 671119
e-mail: mail@holbrooks.com

Contents

Tips & Techniques   **6**

Catherine Wheel   **13**
Catherine Wheel Table Mat   16
Scrappy Zappy Do!   18
Catherine Wheel Combination   23

Jumping Jack   **25**
Criss Cross Stars   30

Trumpet Cracker   **33**
Suffolk Puff   37
Trumpet Cracker Tote   39

Twinkling Star   **43**
Eight Pointed Star Cushion   47
Piping Cushion   48

Fizgig   **51**
Fizgig Whirl   54
Quags, Quillows and Secret Pillows   55

Skyrocket   **61**

Firecracker   **65**

Roman Candle   **69**

Girandole   **75**

Starburst   **81**
Stars for Us   84
Mitred Binding   86

Whirlygig   **89**
Basic Bag   93

Twirling Pinwheel   **95**

Quilt Finale   **99**
Sashing & Corner Squares   101
Scalloped Border   107
Border Corner   109

Glossary & Index   **112**

Kaleidoscopes One: 158 cm (62")
Jennie Rayment
Top row: Fizgig, Skyrocket, Catherine Wheel. Centre row: Twinkling Star, Roman Candle, Starburst.
Bottom row: Trumpet Cracker, Jumping Jack, Girandole. Border: Whirlygig sections and Border Fan.
Created from hand dyed batiks, machine pieced and quilted on polyester batting.

Jennie Rayment

Jennie is internationally renowned for her unusual and novel fabric manipulation techniques. From Origami to fabric sculpture, quilts to garments, her unique designs are for craftswomen and men of any age and ability who are interested in all forms of stitchery. She teaches, lectures and exhibits worldwide. Jennie has written seven books to date and many articles featuring her ingenious constructions. For fact filled and fun demonstrations, educational and very informative workshops, in addition to highly entertaining lectures and presentations, contact Jennie on:

5, Queen Street, Emsworth, Hampshire PO10 7BJ. UK
Tel/fax: + 44 (0) 1243 374860 e-mail; jenrayment@aol.com

www.jennierayment.com

The Beginning

Fizz, bang, wallop, hiss, whiz, the explosive sounds and brilliant flashes of light, mind blowing patterns and ethereal tracery against a dark sky are the elements of every good pyrotechnic display! Enjoying the explosions of colour, shape and form at these events has always been a source of inspiration for me, hence the choice of strong and vibrant hues against a black background - a far cry from my usual calico (muslin in US) heavily manipulated quilts, garments and other artefacts. In keeping with this initial inspiration, each of the twelve ingenious developed blocks is named after one type of pyrotechnic device or another. Some of the designs are completely new and some are re-inventions of traditional patterns, yet all are constructed from simple geometric shapes although tweaked magically to create 3D surface texture. For want of a better description - this is tactile twiddling!

All the blocks are presented in a clear photographic format with each stage of the technique clearly defined and suggestions for further exploration and creative play are included at the end of each chapter. Line drawings are provided so that you can experiment with colour, explore different combinations of tints, tones and shades, and dotted throughout the concise text are helpful hints and useful tips to ensure successful completion of the selected pattern. In addition, throughout the chapters, there are projects to explore from simple bag making, tips on binding and piping plus quags and quilts; indeed within the pages is a wealth of ideas to delight and educate every stitcher of any capability. 'Foldy Rolly Patchwork Pzzazz' sets out to be a comprehensive and clearly written manual for all abilities, and hopes to inspire, develop and improve creative skills in the field of patchwork and surface manipulation.

As many of you are aware this is not my first book but the seventh, and there is more to come! In all the previous publications there were light hearted comments littered throughout the instructions with the occasional amusing anecdote. I have and still do believe in including an element of humour amongst any workshop notes as this produces a modicum of light relief among a series of stolid instructions, so dear reader, please don't be puzzled if you come across some tale or odd comment that makes you smile. Life should not be taken too seriously.

Let's begin your exploration and enjoyment into the world of nipping, tucking, fiddling, twiddling and doubtless lots of rolling and folding with a smile. In the final analysis, as you ponder over the pieces and worry about the accuracy of the seams or whether to trim yet another chunk off the sides to square up the completed creation, do remember that buttons and beads are brilliant and cover up many discrepancies and/or a little extra embroidery enhances and embellishes most excellently!

Calico/Muslin Headboard: 60 x 138 cm (24 x 54")
Jennie Rayment
Trumpet Cracker & Roman Candle with Bias Sashing & Corner Squares, 5 cm (2") border. Machine pieced and quilted.

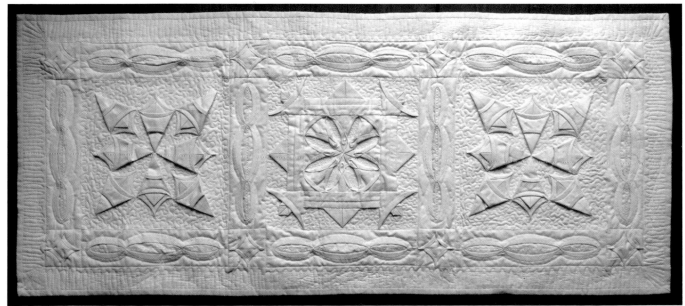

Tips & Techniques

Some of this information you may have read elsewhere or perhaps not. Why not cast a glance over these few pages of helpful hints and practical advice?

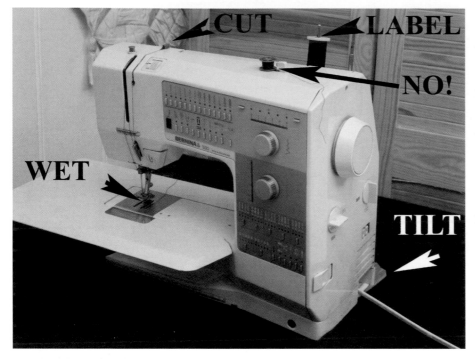

Sewing machine and accessories

Any sewing machine will suffice for the techniques in this book, from a treadle to the latest high-tech all singing and dancing computerised one. A swing-needle model with a range of patterns would be an advantage for decorative stitching, but hand embroidery can be substituted. (On a swing needle machine the needle postion moves from side to side to create width to the stitch.) In addition to the regular presser foot, a ¼" patchwork foot, darning/hopper/free motion foot and an open-toe embroidery foot are useful accessories.

Sewing machine tips

1 Try tilting your sewing machine towards you. If the back edge of the machine is tilted up whilst sewing, the strain on your shoulders is reduced and the overall view of the working surface is greatly improved. You can purchase a tilt table, but two wedge-shaped rubber door stops will work a treat.

2 Do not leave any unused bobbin or thread spool perched anywhere on your machine such as on the spare spindle or parked on the bobbin winder. Just occasionally the loose end of the thread can waft towards the fly wheel and as you continue to sew the reel of thread silently unwinds around the flywheel spindle and into the body of the machine. It is expensive to have miles of tightly wound thread extracted from your machine, especially if it is invisible thread/nylon filament - I know - it has happened to me - twice!

3 Pierce the paper label on the end of the thread spool before putting it onto the thread spindle. This prevents a residue of glue from the label building up on the spindle into a black sticky gunge. Once this occurs the thread spool may not rotate smoothly, as it catches on the residue. In addition, certain machine models have self retracting spindles and once the gunge builds up, the thread spindle may stick down and never return again! White spirit gets the glue off as, amazingly, do baby wipes. (One wonders what they do to the baby! Incidentally, baby wipes also remove dead and dried-on flies from car windscreens and head lights - interesting what can be learnt in a patchwork text book.)

4 Before changing the top thread on the machine, cut the thread just before the tension disc. Remove the reel and pull the remaining section of thread through the needle eye. If you drag the thread off the top of the machine pulling it sharply back through the tension discs, the thread may snag and damage the delicate mechanism of the discs. A little bit of thread is wasted but this in my opinion, this is a sensible way to remove the top thread.

5 For ease of threading the machine, cut the top spool thread end diagonally before you start, this angled cut will thread more easily through the fine needle eye. Now wet the sewing machine needle. If you suck the cut thread end first, it swells and will not fit through the needle eye so easily. Do not bend down and lick the machine needle - the consequences can be dire - simply moisten finger and thumb and damp the needle eye with spit. It works! In addition, a small piece of white card at the back of the needle may help you see the eye more clearly. Of course you can always use the automatic needle threader but if you don't have one and if it doesn't work (a frequent occurrence), try wetting the needle.

Stitch length

The pre-set (2 - 2.5 mm) regular stitch length of many machines is acceptable for seaming two or three layers. Increase the stitch length slightly when sewing multiple layers or stitching through wadding (batting), as the stitch size may contract due to the feed dogs having difficulty in pulling several layers or bulkier materials through evenly.

Needle size

As a general rule, thin and flimsy fabrics need a fine needle e.g. 70 (10 - 11). Thicker fabrics or several layers require a fatter/larger e.g. 90 (14) needle to permit the machine to pierce through the increased depth of fibres. (The needle size increases as the number written on the packet or the needle shank rises - higher nimber = larger needle.)

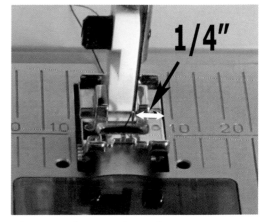

Seam Allowance (S/A)

The usual S/A recommended in many patchwork and quilting books is 0.65 - 0.75 cm (¼"). This is an adequate width for accurate piecing of points and joining of junctions when sewing two layers together. Most sewing machines have a special ¼" foot that you can attach - often referred to as a 'patchwork foot'. You may have one amongst your presser feet or they can be purchased.

Alternatively attach your regular presser foot and try moving the needle position to achieve the selected S/A. Sewing machines with a swing needle (moves side to side) often have a series of different settings for the needle position in relation to the edge of the presser foot. Frequently, in the straight stitch setting, the needle can be shifted by altering the stitch width setting e.g. moving the stitch width setting to 5.5 when in straight stitch mode on many Janome models shifts the needle position to ¼" from the right-hand edge of the regular presser foot. This ability to move the needle and set it at this distance from the right-hand side of the presser foot is advantageous as the regular presser foot can be used. The regular foot has a wide slot unlike the patchwork foot that only has a narrow hole. It is remarkably easy to forget that you have the patchwork foot attached and select a pattern then... Whack... the needle breaks. This may upset the timing on your sewing machine if it happens frequently. The other advantage of using the regular foot and not the patchwork one is that the regular foot sits properly on the feed dogs. Quite a lot of patchwork feet do not cover the feed dogs properly so you don't get the full pulling power of the feed dogs against the base of the presser foot. (For those who don't know what feed dogs are - read your instruction book!)

Shift the needle over towards the right-hand side of the presser foot using the stitch width setting or the needle position lever or dial/knob/button. Check the measurement with an accurate ruler (tape-measures aren't that accurate), and make a note of the setting.

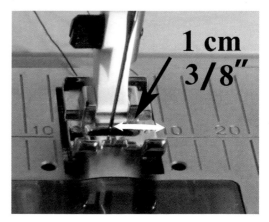

Sometimes in this book a 1 cm (³/₈") S/A is chosen. This wider S/A is selected when piecing a seam consisting of multiple layers of fabric, as all the raw edges may not be accurately aligned. (With a bit of luck and fingers crossed, all layers will be caught in this larger seam.) Do not panic, selecting a different S/A is not difficult. Use the standard presser foot and look on the throat plate (metal plate beneath).

1 cm (³/₈") is often marked on the throat plate. Metric machines may have the plate printed in centimetres or millimetres; consequently 1 cm will be displayed as 1 or 10 (10 mm = 1 cm). Imperial machines (often older models) frequently have their throat plates marked in eighths so ³/₈" is easy to find. Alternatively, move the needle from its central position towards the left-hand side of the presser foot (away from the main body of machine). On most machines the needle will now be 1 cm (³/₈") away from the right-hand edge of the presser foot. Many modern models frequently have several needle positions - check which position provides an accurate 1 cm (³/₈") S/A.

Failing all this, measure 1 cm (³/₈") and rule a line on the fabric.

Basting or Tacking

In Britain, the term 'tacking' normally refers to a series of long stitches (by hand or machine) temporarily holding layers in place. This interpretation is not universal. 'Tacking' in America means stitching all layers together firmly, as we would tack the carpet in place or pin a notice to the board. However, in most parts of the world, basting means a series of long stitches. To prevent any misunderstandings in this text, basting refers to a long stitch length.

For a successful basting stitch, select the longest stitch length (highest number) on the machine and loosen the top tension slightly by turning to a lower number than is reccommended for your normal thread tension. This action should ensure that the bottom bobbin will pull out easily when the basting is removed. Keep the basting close to the raw edges or wherever recommended in the instructions. Pin the layers carefully before commencing. Remove the basting by pulling the bobbin thread.

Sometimes on lowering the presser foot the layers of material shift, even when pinned thoroughly. To prevent this happening, try the following tip.

Lower machine needle into all the layers first before engaging the presser foot. Turn the fly wheel by hand to lower the needle completely through the fabrics then lower the presser foot.

Starting the basting on the fabric with the presser foot and needle holding the layers firm will also help the feed dogs to guide the layers through more evenly.

Basting can always be done by hand if preferred.

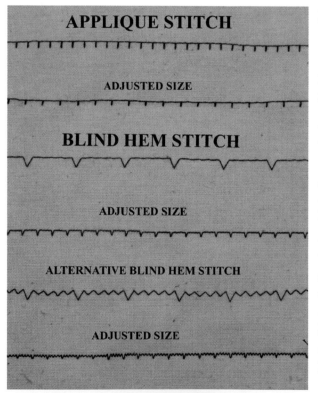

APPLIQUE STITCH

ADJUSTED SIZE

BLIND HEM STITCH

ADJUSTED SIZE

ALTERNATIVE BLIND HEM STITCH

ADJUSTED SIZE

Appliqué/Blind Hem stitches

These stitches are frequently used for securing the edge of a design or shape and when employed carefully give the appearance of very neat hand stitching. Everyone is amazed at your 'hand sewing skills' yet it was machined - it's a fake!

Somewhere in your stitch repertoire there may be one or more of these patterns. To obtain the 'hand-sewn' appearance you may have to alter the stitch settings.

One stitch I frequently use is the 'Blind Hem' stitch pattern which consists of a V shaped bite (indent) with 4 - 5 straight stitches in between. Many machines do this particular stitch but some machines have a variation that would suffice. The other commonly used stitch is labelled an 'Appliqué' stitch and may consist of 2 - 3 straight stitches and a straight bite (indent) not a V shape. This is preferable in many ways to the Blind Hem but not all models have this stitch. Sometimes the Appliqué stitch can be found in the quilting patterns on your sewing machine.

To achieve the 'hand-sewn' effect, adjust the stitch settings then sew carefully along the selected edge. Keep the straight stitching very close to the outside of this edge and just catch the material with the fine 'bite' (indent). Practise first!

An 'open-toed' presser foot gives a clearer view of the edge of the fold than the regular presser foot. Open-toed feet for most models are available from your dealer.

If you are using the Blind Hem pattern do not attach a designated Blind Hem foot - you are not constructing a blind hem but using the stitch as a method of securing an edge.

Use of an invisible thread/nylon filament will ensure that the stitching vanishes even more although a thread well matched to the appliquéd fabric will suffice. If selecting this type of thread the top tension on the machine should be reduced (turn to a lower number). Fill the bottom bobbin with cotton thread preferably, **not** with invisible thread/nylon filament.

Fabric choice

Medium-weight cottons, chintzes (glazed cotton), cretonnes and indeed calico (called muslin in USA) or silk are probably the best choice for the designs in this book. Any fabric type can be used, but crisply finished materials with a firm weave are the easiest to manipulate, and also hold their shape.

Select plain coloured, hand-dyed, batik or tone-on-tone/self patterned materials as opposed to highly patterned fabrics. Stripes work amazingly well as the original pattern distorts when manipulated, thus adding a further design dimension to the overall effect, BUT be very careful when cutting out. Any striped, chequered or indeed directional pattern needs to be very carefully cut and folded in the correct direction or you may find that parts of the completed work are running in the wrong direction or are upside down. This might produce a curious optical effect and have a disturbing appearance, but you may like this!

Washing fabrics

The age old question - to wash fabric beforehand or not? Many people recommend pre-washing of the fabric to remove the problem of any fabric shrinking or the coloured dyes bleeding when you wash your masterpiece in the future. This is an unmitigated nuisance but sensible.

Wash in cool water (the creases won't set so easily), tumble dry or line dry until damp. Press well with either a steam or dry iron (depends on the amount of creasing). Use a spray starch to restore the 'body'. (Starch the material before cutting as the heat of the iron and the moisture from the starch could stretch and distort the pieces.)

If you don't wash the fabric beforehand, to prevent the dyes bleeding and contaminating other colours when the completed item is laundered, try using a 'colour catcher'. This chemically impregnated tissue (available in supermarkets/hardware stores) has the ability to 'catch' stray dye colour and prevent one colour bleeding on to another.

Seam pressing

Pressing all the layers towards the same side of the seam makes one half of the seam very bulky, although the seam junction is supposedly stronger as one layer covers the stitched join. In my opinion, for a more evenly spread seam, press open and flat. In addition a pressed open seam can be informative as you can see the junctions of the previous piecing.

Getting the points accurate

If two or more different shapes have been joined together, when the seam is pressed open on the **W**rong **S**ide (W/S) of the work a small 'V' or maybe a triangle or triangles of different colours may be apparent near the top of the seam. The base of the 'V' or the tips of the triangles indicates the top of the points on the **R**ight **S**ide (R/S).

The next line of stitch must pass exactly past the base of the 'V' or point/s of triangles for accurate piecing.

Technically the distance from the base of the 'V' or triangle tip/s to the raw edge of the fabric should be the selected seam allowance, but due to inaccuracies in any previous stitched seam, this might be different! Mind you, any discrepancies in this measurement are probably due an 'R' in the month, hormones or your age - never due to a deviation from the chosen seam allowance in the first place!

Attaching borders

Measure the width/length of the quilt/hanging/cushion etc. across the centre, or at least several centimetres/inches away from the outside edge. If you measure along the outside edge it might stretch, and this would result in inaccurate measurements. Measuring accurately will produce a finished piece that looks professional, distorted, and uneven borders are not visually pleasing.

There are several ways to attach a border to any square or rectangular piece of work. Some authors favour the 'Log Cabin' method, others like borders with mitred corners; I prefer to use the following three techniques which apply to any desired width of border.

1 Side to side, top and bottom

This is ideally suited for a rectangle as well as a square design. Measure the sides of the work and cut two strips to this measurement. Pin these strips on to the sides W/S up and sew in place. Open out. Press the seams open and flat.

Measure the top and bottom edges and cut two strips to this measurement, pin the strips to the work and sew. Press the seams open and flat.

2 Corner stones

This is best suited for a square block. Why not introduce another colour or different patterned fabric on the corners with this method?

Measure each edge of the block (if all the edges are different - take the average).

Cut four strips at this measurement and four squares the desired width of the border.

Attach the side strips.

Add a square to each end of the top and bottom strips.

Attach these extended pieces to the top and bottom of the work. Match the seams of the corner squares with the side seams - if a little persuasion is required for an accurate match of all the junctions try a good pull or push.

3 Pinwheel/partial seaming

This is an excellent method for bordering a square. It is easy to cut as this natty technique requires four strips the same length. To calculate the length:

A) Measure the block; **deduct the seam allowance** e.g. 0.75 cm (¼″) from all sides to get the finished measurement. (This is the measurement after the outside edge has been seamed.)

B) Decide on the finished width of the border.

The length of the strips is the finished measurement of the block (A) plus the finished width of the border (B) <u>plus seam allowances on all sides</u>.

Therefore a 30 cm (**12″**) finished block with a 5 cm (**2″**) finished border requires four strips 35 cm (**14″**) long x 5 cm (**2″**) wide **PLUS** the relevant seam allowances e.g. 0.75 cm (¼″) added to all sides. Consequently four 36.5 cm (**14½″**) x 6.5 cm (**2½″**) strips will be cut.

Line up the first strip <u>with the right-hand edge</u> of the bottom of the block. Start the sewing approximately 10 cm (**4″**) from the bottom of the block, leaving much of the strip unattached. Sew to the bottom.

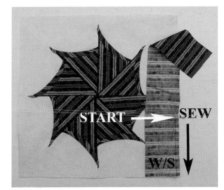

Fold the strip outwards. Working anti/counterclockwise, turn the block to the next side and attach the second strip. Pin the strip in place at both ends and sew the entire length.

Add the remaining two strips in the same manner working round the block anti/counterclockwise. Each strip should fit exactly from one end of the block to the other, if not, check your mathematics!

Complete the stitching by turning the block round and finishing the first seam. Leaving a long section of the first strip unattached now proves useful because you can ease the strip to fit the side.

If you've read this chapter, well done! Reading basic 'destructions' is boring but you never know - there might be a pearl of wisdom among them that might just help you.

Traumatic Travels of a Tucked-up Twiddler

For my sins, I seem to spend a fair bit of time flying round the globe teaching and prattling to a variety of different audiences. As I only do 'Show and Tell', this means humping two big bags full of lesson preparation, quilts and other assorted samples of my craft.

Over the years I have learnt quite a lot about travelling and seemingly always the hard way. This is probably due to rushing around like a headless chicken and not stopping to think. Travel is supposed to broaden the mind and open one's eyes to new experiences. Some of these I could have done without...

Doors abroad!

How could anyone find a problem with a door - it opens and closes? Well, wait until you have arrived at an elevator (lift in UK), put some of your baggage in, turned round to collect next bag then found the elevator has departed behind your back to another floor. What about waltzing through to the terraced garden carrying your plate of breakfast to discover a plate glass door in the way? Head meeting door causes large lump on brow and breakfast dish meeting floor makes a lovely sticky mess. (Why wasn't there a notice or indication that the exit to the patio was filled with a sparkling clean glass door? A few grubby hand-prints would have alerted me.)

On my very first trip overseas, I learnt a salutary lesson about US doors. A vast pile of photocopying had to be done for my classes and I had spotted a copy place on my morning run round the locality. It opened at 9.00 a.m.

Having arrived outside the store at 9.00 a.m. exactly clutching my top copies, all the lights were on so I pushed the door but it remained shut - still locked I assumed. No matter, a quick trot round the block and they would surely be open. Returning five minutes later, there were people inside but door was still firmly shut. Obviously a staff training day or something like that or so I thought and decided to go round the block again. Back once more and still the door would not open so I knocked somewhat peremptorily on the glass. A young man came up to the door and opened it outwards onto the street. "Ma'm, were you trying to get in?" he asked politely. How was I to know that doors to stores in the US open outwards into the street?

But the worst door disaster was a few months ago... 4.30 a.m. and I was leaving the hotel room to go to the airport - my cab was due in a few minutes. For some reason, I left my key in the room, pushed my bags into the corridor and let the door shut behind me. What I did not appreciate that most of my frilly handkerchief-hemmed skirt had remained behind and was firmly trapped between the door and the surrounding wood-work. There was no way, I could move. The choice was to try to clamber out of my skirt and go to reception to get another key (in my underwear) so I could open the door and release the garment or try to wriggle the skirt out of the door jamb. Fifteen minutes later, hot, sweaty and pink faced with the effort, wriggling the fabric eventually worked. Fortunately the cab driver was still waiting and I managed to catch the plane albeit by the skin of my teeth, but at least fully dressed.

Travel is such fun!

Catherine Wheel

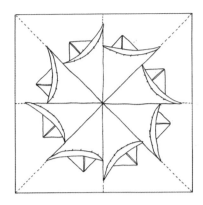

31.5 cm (**12½″**) including outer S/A

Cut

Two 15 cm (**6″**) squares - **Red** (*Cut each square in half diagonally, making two triangles*)
Two 15 cm (**6″**) squares - **Green** (*Cut each square in half diagonally, making two triangles*)
Four 17.5 cm (**6 ⁷/₈″**) squares - **Black** (*Cut each square in half diagonally, making two triangles*)
Eight 7.5 cm (**3″**) squares - **Yellow**

Start Stitching

Seam Allowance 0.75 cm (**¼″**)

1 Fold and press one **Red** triangle in half diagonally, R/S out.

2 Place one **Black** triangle - R/S up. Lay the folded and pressed **Red** triangle on top as shown in the diagram. Align all raw edges.

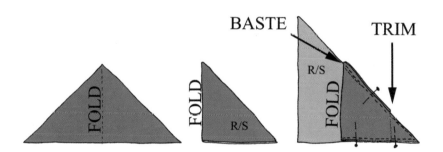

Trim the underside of the red triangle where indicated by the arrow. This will reduce the bulk in the finished centre seams - not trimming might make the centre lumpy, and you don't want that!

Pin both the shapes together. Baste the **Red** triangle to the **Black** one - use the longest stitch length and keep the basting within the 0.75 cm (**¼″**) seam allowance.

3 Make three more sections using the three remaining **Red** and **Black** triangles.

Check all four sections are identical otherwise the end result may be a different design.

4 Fold and press one **Green** triangle diagonally in half - R/S out. Arrange on another **Black** triangle as shown in the diagram. Trim part of the underside of the **Green** triangle as indicated by the arrow. Pin both shapes together and baste in place.

Make three more with remaining **Green** and **Black** triangles.

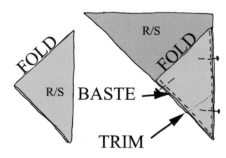

13

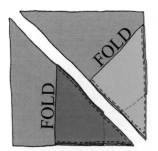

5 Take one basted triangle of each colour. Arrange as in the diagram. Place both sections R/S together aligning the raw edges. Pin the layers. Sew the diagonal edge (bias) using 0.75 cm (¼″) S/A. Press seam the open and flat.

Be careful not to stretch the bias edge. Pin carefully before sewing.

6 Repeat Stage 5 three more times making four squares. Lay out the squares as shown above.

7 Sew two squares together to form one half of the block. Repeat with the other two squares. Press the seam open and flat.

8 Sew both halves together. Endeavour to match the points of the **Red** and **Green** triangles at the centre but don't fret too much - this design could so easily be embellished with a button.

Look carefully at the seam - there should be a small 'V' visible in the seam. (The base of the 'V' is indicated by the arrow.) If you sew through the base of this 'V' then the points of the shapes should be accurate on the R/S of the block - one lives in hope!

9 Press all seams open and flat and trim the 'ears' off the outside corners of the block. Remove any basting that shows on the front of the work.

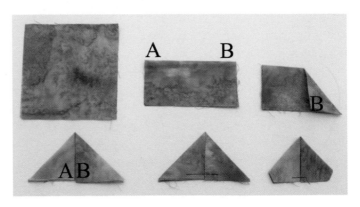

10 Fold one 7.5 cm (3″) **Yellow** square in half R/S out. Press the fold.

11 Work from the folded edge; fold both **A** and **B** corners over to form a triangle. Baste across the bottom of the triangle to anchor the folds. Trim both corners off the triangle.

12 Make seven more identical triangles using the remaining 7.5 cm (**3"**) squares.

13 Insert the trimmed **Yellow** triangles into the pockets behind the **Red** and **Green** sections. Tuck each shape in until only 1 cm (**½"**) of the tip of the triangle shows. Pin the triangle in place.

Try to position the inserts accurately. The completed block looks better if they are all at the same angle and the same distance from the seam, unless you prefer otherwise! (This particular method of folding a square is often referred to as Somerset or Folded Patchwork.)

14 Roll back the edge of the pocket. Stitch in place using a small hand slip stitch (a thimble may be necessary) and sew through all the layers. For those to whom hand-sewing is an anathema, use the sewing machine - see page 8 for suggested stitches.

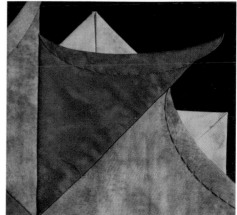

There is no reason why the rolled edge can't be secured at intervals to retain both the inserted shape and keep the edge rolled back. Do you have to sew all the way along? No, but it might be sensible to do some stitching to prevent the **Yellow** insert falling out.

Play Time

How about padding the pockets and omitting the textural inserts? Lightly stuff the pockets with some toy filling/torn up bits of polyester wadding or any other washable padding fibre. Push the fibres down well, and then roll back the pocket edge in an arc. Pin in place before sewing through all the layers to retain the filling. Do not over stuff with the chosen fibre as this can cause distortion of the fabric.

Do you have to roll the folded edge? No! Leave the fold lying in a straight line. Sew the edge in place - sew through all the layers.

Why not have both padded pockets and textural inserts? Go for maximum effect! Bit of stuffing does no-one any harm.

Try the pattern in stripes - on rolling back the edge of the pockets, the striped pattern will distort and create an interesting optical illusion. Replace part of the block with stripy fabric or go crazy and make the entire piece with stripes going every which way.

Alternatively, use a sheer material such as a net/lace/organza to make the pockets then the background material will show through. If the block is not going to be washed, contemplate padding the pockets with lavender or pot-pourri. You could have a touchy-feely smelly Catherine Wheel! Wow!!

Catherine Wheel Table Mat

30 cm (**12"**) diameter

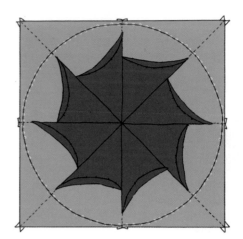

Materials

One completed Catherine Wheel block without inserts
32 cm (**13"**) square wadding/batting or heat resistant fabric
32 cm (**13"**) square backing fabric
110 x 6.5 cm (**43 x 2½"**) bias cut strip (See page 101 for advice on ruler position when bias cutting)
Compass/30 cm (**12"**) diameter object such as a plate

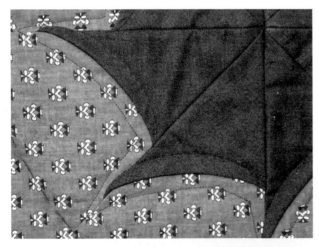

1 Draw a circle on the block:
Set a compass at 15 cm (**6"**) radius; insert point of compass into centre of the design and draw a 30 cm (**12"**) circle on the Catherine Wheel block. Alternatively find a 30 cm (**12"**) diameter object, lay it on top and draw round the edge. (Near enough to this measurement is acceptable - it is not that important to have a circle exactly this diameter.)

2 Press the block well. Lay the block R/S up onto the wadding (don't add the backing material at this stage). Pin the layers together on the four corners.

3 Stitch approximately 0.75 cm (**¼"**) round the outside edge of the central design. Use the edge of the presser foot as a guide - follow the outline of the design with the edge of presser foot. Choose to work with the needle in the regular position (in the centre of the presser foot) or move the needle position to 0.75 cm (**¼"**) from left-hand side of presser foot.

4 Lay the stitched block on the backing fabric and pin the layers well. Sew round the drawn circular line using a walking foot or a darning/hopper/free motion foot (use of the regular straight stitch foot may cause one of the layers to 'creep'), or sew together by hand. (Perish the thought!!) Cut off all excess material back to the stitched line to form a circle.

5 Finally, bind the raw outer edge with the bias cut strip.

Binding a Circle

Fold the bias strip in half and press. Align the raw edges of the folded bias strip EXACTLY with the stitched drawn line round the outside of the mat. Begin the stitching approximately 7 cm (**3″**) from start of the pressed bias strip. Don't worry about this unattached floppy length of binding, the floppy bit will be useful when joining the ends together. Sew binding in place using a 0.75 cm (¼″) S/A.

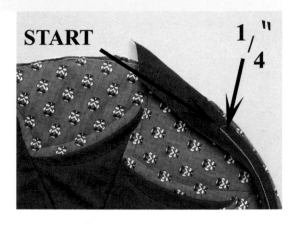

Stop sewing about 9 cm (**3½″**) away from the start point of the stitching.

Open out the 'floppy' section of the bias strip (the length left unattached at the start) and fold the diagonally cut end 0.75 cm (¼″) over to the W/S of the bias strip.

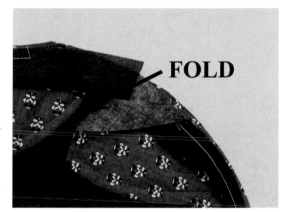

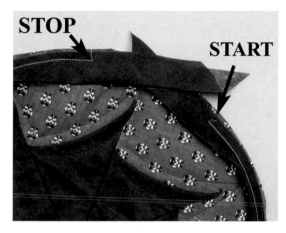

Lay the end of the bias strip inside the 'floppy' section.

Fold the 'floppy' end over and sew straight past.

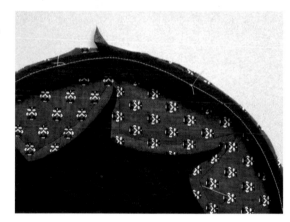

Fold the edge of the bias strip carefully over the raw edge of the table mat. Pin in place.

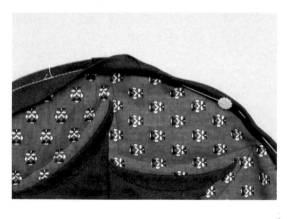

Now turn the mat over and slip stitch the folded edge of the bias strip in place on the back.

Now you have made one table mat, you will have to make some more - guess who's coming to dinner? Sadly, I suspect Spencer Tracey, Katherine Hepburn and Sidney Poitier might not be but you and your friends will appreciate them.

Scrappy Zappy Do!

63 x 107 cm (**25 x 42"**)

Gather up the scraps and get ready to play. Twenty different coloured batiks set on a black background were used in this design.

How about using one colour instead of twenty different ones and graduating the shades?

Arrange your colour selection from light to dark or vice versa. As it can be difficult to select which shade/tint or tone is lighter or darker, use a black and white photocopier. Photocopying the materials will produce a range of greys. This makes it much easier to arrange your selection in the right order.

For those who like simplicity, make the pattern in just two fabrics - one for the background and one for the curving design and striped border. (Much simpler to prepare - there's no frantic searching through your scrap stash and agonising over which colours to choose.)

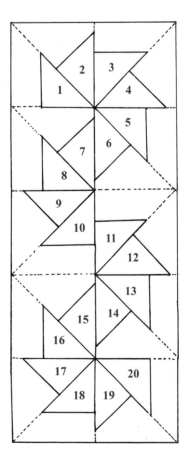

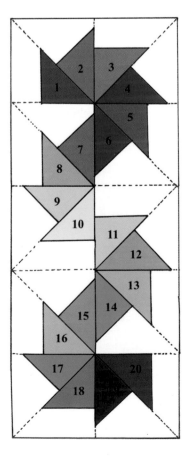

One last suggestion: Why not 'Follow the Rainbow' by arranging the colours from Red through to Blue and Violet? If you can't remember in what order the colours occur - that good old mnemonic '**R**ichard **O**f **Y**ork **G**ave **B**attle **I**n **V**ain' is a good reminder. (Red, Orange, Yellow, Green, Blue, Indigo and Violet).

Colour in the diagram to produce a rough sketch of the completed piece. This helps to indicate the position of each fabric.

Once you have sorted out the colours, gather up the fabrics and begin cutting out. As you cut, number the pieces to match the diagram. Why, you might ask? The reason is very simple - the entire design can go totally pear-shaped if you don't and you wouldn't want a pear shape - would you? Surely it is more of a wiggle!

For ease of construction cut twenty 15 cm (6") squares - one from each selected colour then cut each square in half diagonally to form two triangles. You will end up with forty triangles... but... you can always make another Scrappy Zappy Do with the leftover ones!

Alternatively use one of the many templates available to cut 'half square' triangles. Please remember to press the fabric before you start cutting. In addition, should you wish to spray the material with starch, treat the fabric first before cutting into the desired shape.

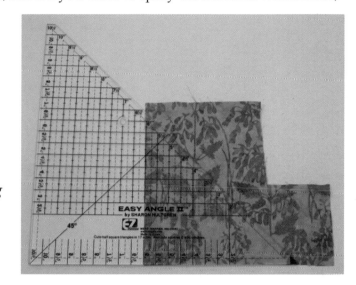

Cut a right angled corner before cutting a 6" half square triangle. Align the edge of the template and 6" measurement (marked on template) with this right angled cut edge.

Word of warning - PLEASE read the start of this chapter from page 13 then you might have a rough idea of the construction technique - all this leaping into the middle of any chapter and guessing the method doesn't always work!

Materials
Twenty 15 x 15 cm (**6 x 6"**) half square triangles - **Colour**
OR Ten 15 cm (**6"**) squares - **Colour** *(Cut each square in half diagonally, making two triangles)*
Ten 17.5 cm (**6⅞"**) squares - **Black** *(Cut each square in half diagonally, making two triangles)*
75 x 115 cm (**30 x 44"**) - **Black** borders and binding
Oddments of fabric for striped border **OR** Three 5 x 115 cm (**2 x 44"**) strips (See Striped Border page 21)
65 x 105 cm (**26 x 44"**) rectangle backing fabric
65 x 105 cm (**26 x 44"**) rectangle wadding

Start Stitching
Seam Allowance 0.75 cm (¼")

1 Press each **Colour** triangle in half.

2 Lay the pressed triangles in desired colour order. Arrange the shapes with all the folds on the **RIGHT-HAND** side. Now **NUMBER** the pieces as shown below!

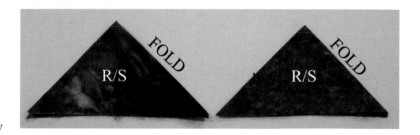

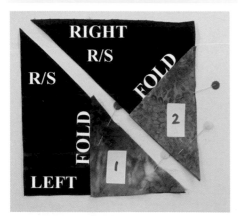

3 Take two **Black** triangles and arrange to form a square. Pin **Colour** #1 triangle to a left-hand section. Pin **Colour** #2 triangle to right-hand section.

As it is so easy to get in a huge muddle with the colour arrangement follow the next steps without querying - just do it!

4 Pin **Colour** triangles #3, 5, 8, 10, 11, 13, 16, 18 and 20 to a **LEFT-**hand positioned **Black** triangle.

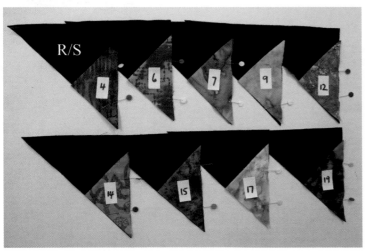

5 Pin **Colour** triangles #4, 6, 7, 9, 12, 14, 15, 17 and 19 to a **RIGHT-**hand positioned **Black** triangle as shown above.

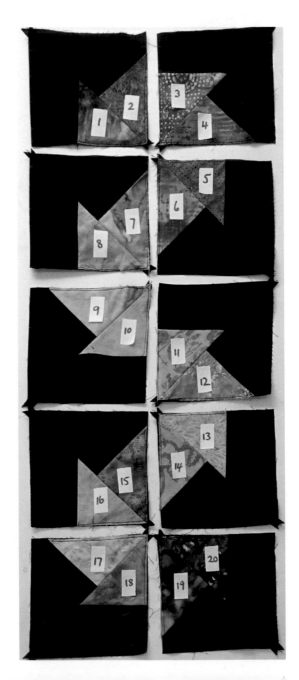

6 Lay out all the sections and check that you have everything in the correct colour order. Trim the underside of the **Colour** triangles (Stage 2 page 13). Baste the **Colour** triangles to the **Black** ones along the raw edges.

7 Sew each left hand section to each right-hand section forming a square (Stage 5 page 20). Make sure that the numbers are in the correct places.

8 Sew the squares together. Start by sewing two squares together to form a short row. Press the seam open and flat.

9 Sew the short rows of squares into larger sections. Press all seams open and flat.

10 Sew larger sections together to form the complete panel. Press as above.

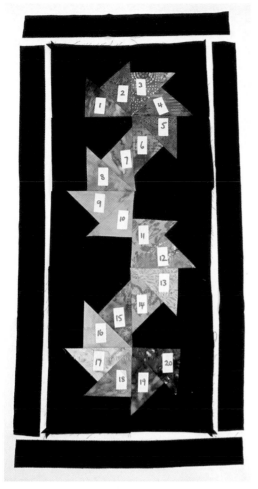

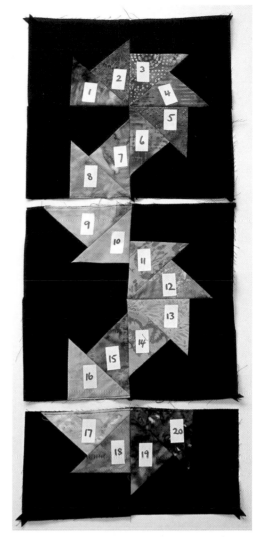

11 Measure the sides of the panel and cut two 5 cm (**2"**) wide **Black** strips this length. Attach to the sides. Press.

12 Measure across the top and the bottom. Cut two strips to this measurement and attach. Press well.

13 Now… remove the numbers from the completed panel.

Striped Border

Ignore these instructions if you are only working in two colours - it would be a trifle silly to cut strips in the same colour, sew together then cut up again! Use the 5 x 115 cm (**2 x 44"**) strips for this border instead of cutting up lots of scraps and sewing these together.

1 From the oddments of material, cut different widths of strips approximately 50 cm (**20"**) long. Sew these together in a specific order or throw them up in the air and arrange them randomly. Your choice - you are the artiste!

Join the strips together to make a striped band 25 cm (**10"**) deep or thereabouts. Press the seams open and flat.

2 Trim the end of the stitched striped band. Cut approximately eleven 4 cm (**1½"**) wide strips working from this cut end.

3 Join several strips into two lengths that will fit the sides of the panel. Attach one to each side. Join more strips to fit the top and bottom. Sew in place.

4 For the final border, cut 10 cm (**4"**) **Black** strips and attach.

5 Roll back the edges of the **Colour** sections and stitch in place (Stage 14, page 15).

6 Place the completed panel on the wadding and backing fabric. Baste the layers before commencing any quilting. Complete the project with a Mitred Binding (page 86).

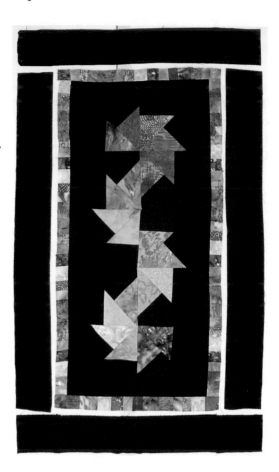

For extra pzzazz and a bit of embellishment, when quilting the panel, why not stitch round the outside of the central design with a variegated thread?

Catherine Wheel Combination

85 x 85 cm (**33½ x 33½"**)

This small hanging or cot quilt features one complete Catherine Wheel block in the centre and three quarters of four other Catherine Wheel blocks surrounding it.

The marvellous marbled fabrics in this creation were designed by Quilters Treasure, New Hampshire, USA. (www.quilterstreasure.com)

Materials

Centre: One **Turquoise** & **Cream** Catherine Wheel (pages 13 - 15)
Twelve 15 cm (**6"**) squares - **Green** (*Cut each square in half diagonally, making two triangles*)
Twelve 17.5 (**6⁷/₈"**) squares - **Cream** (*Cut each square in half diagonally, making two triangles*)
Twelve 7.5 (**3"**) squares - **Turquoise**
75 x 115 cm (**30 x 44"**) - **Black** border and binding
75 x 115 cm (**30 x 44"**) - **Brown** border
65 x 105 cm (**26 x 42"**) backing fabric and 65 x 105 cm (**26 x 42"**) wadding

1 Follow Stages 1 - 14 pages 13 - 15 to make the centre section.

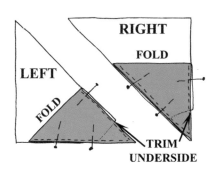

2 Now for the surrounding sections: Ah-ha! Watch the next bit... the **Green** folded triangles are laid onto the **Cream** background in the reverse direction to the centre ones - forming a mirror image of the centre block folded triangles. Confused? Yes!

Panic not! All you have to do is make the sections up as shown in the left-hand diagrams.

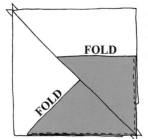

Don't trim the underside of the Green folded triangles before you have checked that they lie in the same position as shown on the diagram.

3 Sew both sections to form a square. Make eleven more sections the same.

4 Arrange all twelve sections round the centre block. Sew the two side sections together and attach to the centre block.

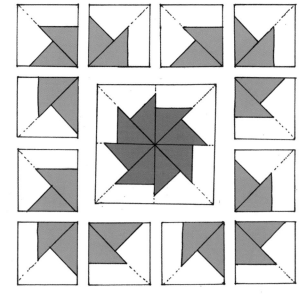

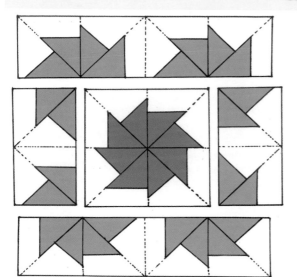

5 Stitch all four top and bottom sections together and attach.

6 Add a 3 cm (1¼") **Black** border to all four sides.

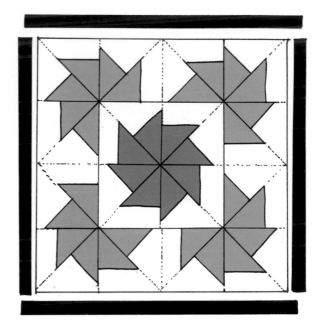

7 Add a 11 cm (4½") **Brown** border to all four sides.

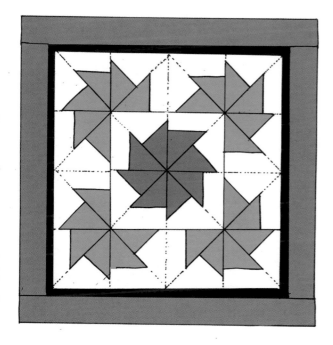

8 Fold all the **Turquoise** squares into triangles (Stages 10 - 11, page 14) and insert. Roll back all the folded edges of all the **Green** and **Turquoise** sections and sew in place.

9 Mount the panel onto wadding and backing fabric. Baste layers before quilting.

The central section of this Catherine Wheel Combination was free-motion quilted using a basic 'wiggle' usually referred to as stippling.

On the outer border, I used a curved pattern which I believe was first developed by Katherine McTavish. This consists of a series of connected arcs of differing sizes.

10 Bind the panel with remaining **Black** fabric (for Mitred Binding see page 86).

Jumping Jack

31.5 cm (**12½″**) including outer S/A

Cut

Four 6.5 cm (**2½″**) squares - **Green**
Eight 6.5 x 11.5 cm (**2½ x 4½″**) strips - **Orange**
Four 12.5 cm (**4⁷/₈″**) squares - **Black**
Four 6.5 cm (**2½″**) squares - **Black**

Eight 6.5 cm (**2½″**) squares - **Yellow**
Two 15 cm (**6″**) squares - **Purple**
Four 6.5 x 11.5 cm (**2½ x 4½″**) strips - **Black**

Start Stitching

Seam Allowance 0.75 cm (**¼″**)

1 Press one 6.5 cm (**2½″**) **Yellow** square in half diagonally forming a triangle, R/S out.

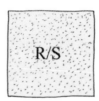 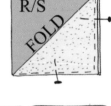

2 Pin and baste one **Yellow** triangle onto one **Black** 6.5 cm (**2½″**) square. Repeat with the remaining three **Yellow** triangles and **Black** squares. Keep the basting close to the raw edge.

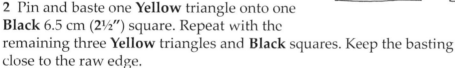

3 Arrange these squares as a pin wheel and sew together. Sew two squares together first to form one half of the completed design. Repeat with remaining two squares. Press seams open and flat.

4 Join both halves R/S together to form a square. Try to match the points of the triangles in the centre.

With luck the points will touch at the centre but...

A button covers most discrepancies in any seam junction. Also... being a 'Mrs Picky Pants' and always aiming for perfection can be most wearisome! (Overheard this nickname when one of my students referred to her friend as being such a person.)

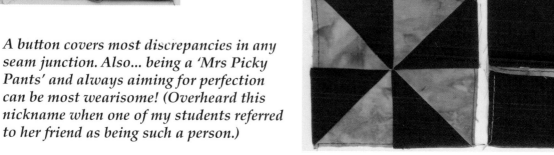

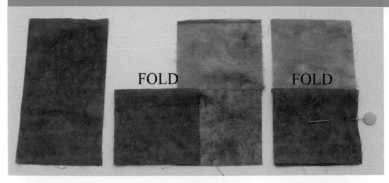

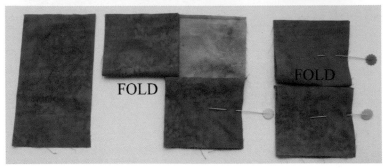

5 Sew one 6.5 cm (2½″) **Green** square to one 6.5 cm (2½″) **Yellow** square. Press seam open and flat.

6 Fold one 6.5 x 11.5 cm (2½ x 4½″) **Orange** rectangle in half. Align the folded edge of the **Orange** rectangle precisely with the seam between the **Yellow** and **Green** squares. Pin in place.

7 Fold another **Orange** rectangle in half. Align the folded edge of this **Orange** rectangle precisely with the seam between the **Yellow** and **Green** squares.

Both folded edges of the rectangles are aligned **EXACTLY** on the seam. Pin in place.

8 Baste the folded rectangles on the right-hand edge to keep them in place. Keep the basting within the seam allowance.

9 Lay one 5 x 11.5 cm (2½ x 4½″) **Black** strip on top and sew the **RIGHT-HAND** side.

Consistency is the key! At all times have the Yellow square at the top when you attach the Black strip and sew the RIGHT-HAND side otherwise the completed design may not resemble the photographs. BE CAREFUL!

10 Press the seam open and flat. The rounded ends of the **Orange** rectangles should be pressed as shown in the picture.

11 Repeat Stages 5 - 10 three more times.

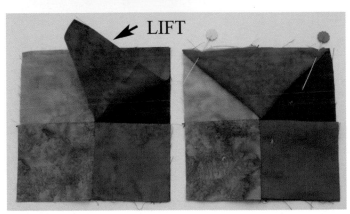

12 Turn the block over to the R/S and lift one of the **Orange** rectangles.

Open the piece out and arrange to form a triangle. Pin the corners of the triangle in place. Jiggle the shape until the corners of the **Orange** triangle bisect the corners of the **Black** and **Yellow** squares.

13 Repeat with the other rectangle. Once opened and pinned in place - baste bottom! (No - not yours, but the bottom of each triangle.) Keep basting close to raw edge.

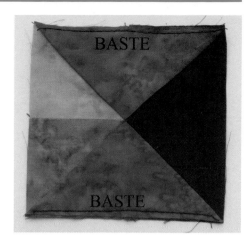

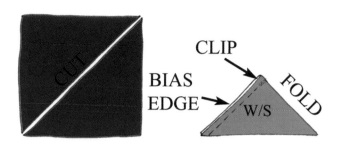

14 Cut one **Purple** 15 cm (6″) square in half diagonally. Fold each triangle on diagonal (R/S inside).

15 Look carefully - sew the **BIAS** edge of each triangle (that's the stretchiest side). It is very easy to sew the wrong side of the triangle whilst being distracted. (Stop multi-tasking! Forget about what you are going to have for supper - concentrate!)

Take care not to stretch the bias edge when sewing or pressing.

16 Clip the corner off the top of the seam. Open out the triangle and flatten the shape into a square. Press the seam open. Turn the shape R/S out and arrange into a TRIANGLE. Press gently.

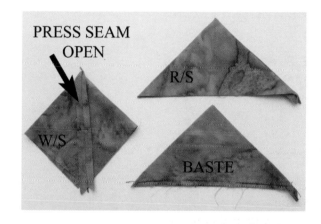

Use the blunt end of a barbecue skewer to poke the top corner of the triangle out - if you use the sharp end you may make a hole in the material.

17 Cut one **Black** 12.5 cm (4⅞″) square in half diagonally forming two triangles. Lay one triangle R/S up. Place one **Purple** triangle on the **Black** triangle as shown aligning all raw edges. There must be a 0.75 cm (¼″) gap between the base of the **Purple** triangle and the raw edge of the **Black** one. The seam of the **Purple** triangle is on the left-hand side.

Watch that little 'nose' sticking out of the end of the Purple triangle - it should be a short distance from the TOP of the Black triangle. If the 'nose' is 0.75 cm (¼″) from the bottom of the Black triangle - turn the shape round as it will be the wrong way up in the completed block and the final appearance of the Jumping Jack block will be different.

18 Lay another **Black** triangle on top sandwiching the **Purple** triangle R/S together. Sew down diagonal - bias edge. Try not to stretch this edge as you stitch.

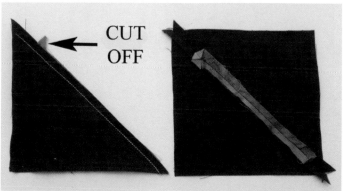

19 On completion, clip the end of the **Purple** 'nose' from the seam. Press the seam open and flat. Press the ends of the **Purple** insert inwards.

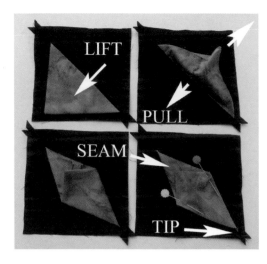

20 Lift the **Purple** triangle up and pull the sides apart. It will flatten into a diamond shape with a centre flap. Fold the centre flap back so that it partially covers the seam. Pin the shape in place and press gently.

21 Make three more sections.

Now for the interesting part - sew the pieces together.

22 Arrange all the sections as shown.

Look at the photograph - it is very easy to get the squares with the Purple diamonds the wrong way round. The tip of the Purple diamond should be towards the centre (see the arrow).

23 Sew the sections together as shown above. Press all seams open and flat. Remove any basting that shows on the front. Trim the 'ears' from the seams once the seam is stitched. Match all points where possible - a bit of pulling and pushing of the various layers can be most advantageous! Press well and check the size. It should measure 31.5 cm (**12½″**) square, if it doesn't then check the accuracy of your seam allowance. Hacking lumps off the edges to make the block the right size might not be a good idea as you will loose the points in the outside seams (see page 45). Trim all ears from the outer edges.

Now you can fiddle with the folded edges. Roll, fold, nip and tuck where you like - the choice is yours. Alternatively, follow the suggestions below.

1 Roll back and pin down all the folded edges of the **Yellow** and **Orange** sections. Some fabrics will roll more easily than others - roll back the edge until the block surface starts to distort. If distortion occurs, release the fold until the block lies flat again.

2 Sew round edges of rolled back folds using one of the appliqué stitches (page 8) or a small slip stitch by hand (perish the thought!).

Invisible thread/nylon filament is a good choice as it saves changing thread colour each time you move to a different fabric. Remember to loosen the top tension a little (turn to a lower number) to prevent the bottom bobbin thread showing on the top. Another word of warning - do not press with a hot iron as the invisible thread may melt.

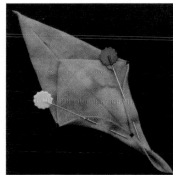

3 Stabilise the corners of the **Purple** diamonds with a few small stitches. Roll the outer edges together. Where the two folded edges touch, secure the layers with a stitch or two.

Add a little extra twiddling by rolling the folds at the end of the diamond back again to form a small petal shape. Secure the sides with stitches.

If the end product is to have heavy use - stitch the folds securely to retain the shape.

Playtime

Why not make another one and re-arrange the centre pieces forming a square and not a pin wheel. An easier option as you don't have to match the points of the triangles in the centre. Bet you wished you had seen this page first!

Criss Cross Stars

137 x 198 cm (**54 x 78″**)

Why not combine Catherine Wheels and Jumping Jacks? The centre panel of this delightful single bed quilt is constructed from eight Catherine Wheel and seven Jumping Jack blocks with the addition of a few extra squares folded into triangles. These triangles link the blocks together to form the criss cross. The scalloped border is created from the Twirling Pinwheel design (page 95).

Centre panel

1 Make eight Catherine Wheel blocks (pages 13 - 15) and seven Jumping Jacks (pages 25 - 29) BUT be aware that colour placement of the pieces in the middle of the Jumping Jack block has been slightly altered. In addition the pieces of the centre block of the quilt have been arranged as depicted in the alternative design shown on page 29 and the colour arrangement slightly adjusted. Why not play and see what pattern you can create by moving the colours around?

2 Cut sixteen **Purple** 9.5 cm (3¾″) squares. Press in half R/S out forming triangles.

3 These triangles are placed on the corners of the Catherine Wheel blocks and basted in place. Keep the basting within the 0.75 cm (¼″) S/A.

Beware: not all the blocks have a square on every corner - only two do! There are four Catherine Wheel blocks with one triangle basted on one corner and two blocks with two corners with a basted triangle.

Follow the diagram above to get the triangles in the right places.

4 Sew all fifteen blocks together to make the centre panel.

To increase the size of the quilt, add borders:
Cut six 4.5 cm (1¾") **Cream** strips for the first border. For the second border cut six 6 cm (2¼") **Mid Purple** strips. With luck and fingers crossed, once both borders have been attached the quilt should measure 166.5 x 106.5 cm (**66½ x 42½"**).

The zigzag border is constructed from thirty-six Twirling Pinwheel sections (page 95). Making all these sections is a bit like being in a sweat-shop - why not skip this bit? Simply finish off the quilt with a binding or add another border and then bind. For those of you game to continue - once the thirty-six sections have been constructed, join eleven sections together for each side and seven sections together for the top and bottom forming four long strips.

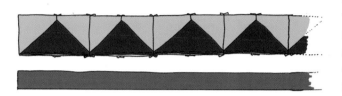

Increase the width of these strips by attaching a 4 cm (1½") strip (striped fabric in photograph).

Add the side strips to the quilt. Then attach the corner block to each end of the two remaining strips. The corner block is created from one **Purple** and one **Green** 11.5 (4") square. The **Purple** square is folded in half diagonally and basted to the **Green** as explained in Stage 1 page 25.

Finally cut seven 9 cm (3½") **Mid Purple** strips for the last border and attach. Mount the completed quilt top onto wadding/batting with a backing fabric, quilt the layers in your preferred style, bind and enjoy!

For a smaller quilt, ideal as a lap quilt or for a small child, make five Jumping Jacks and four Catherine Wheels. Add two 9.5 cm (3¾") squares pressed in half to form triangles to each Catherine Wheel block. Arrange as shown below on the left.

Alternatively, why not create a subtly different effect with four Jumping Jacks and five Catherine Wheels as depicted in the right.

You will need eight 9.5 cm (3¾") squares to complete this arrangement.

The choice is yours!

Cops and Robbers

For some unfathomable reason, in 2010, I decided that I would run in the London Marathon. This feat as I am but a somewhat half-hearted morning trotter of a mile or two would require my feet to be comfortably shod with correctly fitted running shoes.

Now this is a cautionary tale so take note dear Reader. In pursuit of my comfy shoes, I went back to a local Sports shop. This family run emporium has a staff of particularly pleasant young men, who feel your toes, fiddle with your ankles and find you new shoes which they lace with due tenderness to your feet. Bliss. I was attentively fitted and then dispatched to try them out. Dutifully, I abandoned my coat and bag and trotted off down the road. Alas, the shoes were most uncomfortable so it was a quick nip back to store in the hope of finding same young man to re-fit my feet. Imagine my horror on returning to my seat, I stared at my heap of belongings and discovered that my bag which had been firmly zippered up beforehand was now open and my purse was missing. Panicked, I squealed and squeaked "My purse has gone!" but to no avail - not a soul acknowledged my distress nor proffered any help. Glancing round I saw two large men standing near the entrance, one of whom was stuffing his hand down his trouser front. In an instant, I knew where my purse was - down his trousers.

Now, a well brought up lass doesn't accost a strange man and ask to search inside his trousers so I was somewhat fazed. As I stood, expostulating about my lack of purse, they turned and went rapidly out of the store. Once the door slid behind them, a young girl said "I saw that man take your purse!" She then explained what she had seen - I had been right. How dare any one pinch my purse - I wasn't going to accept this lying down? No, I was going to get it back. My personal life was in that purse, my driving licence, credit and store loyalty cards, my library ticket and more. Hurling myself down the road, I shrieked at their retreating bodies "I know you have my purse, keep the money but please let me have it back!" (Why did I say please?) To my utter astonishment, they dropped the purse on the pavement. Arriving at the abandoned object, a quick flick ensured that all the personal stuff was there - the money had gone. Not a real catastrophe, but among the coins lay my silver St Christopher. This medal goes everywhere with me - they weren't having it!

Down the road I went again, now shouting "Keep the money but can I have my St Christopher back please." Once more they threw something on the pavement just before they turned up a side alley. Sweating profusely (sorry, ladies glow), I galloped up to the spot. Yes, there it lay - a small round silver medal. I had it back. Breathlessly, I returned to the store. The police had arrived, called no doubt by some responsible citizen. "Madam", said one burly helmeted copper, "I gather there has been an incident. Can you give me a description of the man involved?" No! I could describe what his trousers were made of, the length and make of the zip and how many buttons there were but his face? I never looked at his face - all I was interested in was what he had stuffed in his trousers!

Moral of this tale is never leave your personal belongings in the public view and if you do get robbed - take a note of the facial appearance of the thieves, this might help catch them as police records do not usually list the exact specifications of the criminal's trousers. Finally, for those who like to know all the details - yes, I did buy the shoes, they can't have been as uncomfortable as I thought as I didn't notice any pain when I chased the thieves and they seemed to be lucky and yes; I did complete the marathon in a reasonable time for a novice.

Trumpet Cracker

31.5 cm (**12½″**) including outer S/A

Cut
Four 18.5 cm (**7¼″**) squares - **Black**
Four 14.5 cm (**5¾″**) squares - **Green**
Four 14.5 cm (**5¾″**) squares - **Red**
Eight 7.5 cm (**3″**) squares - **Yellow**

Start Stitching
Seam Allowance 1 cm (³/₈″)

1 Gently finger press one **Green**
14.5 cm (**5¾″**) square in half on the
diagonal forming a triangle, R/S outside.
Fold shape again to make smaller triangle.
One side of the triangle has two folds,
ensure that the two folds are flush. Pin the
layers together.

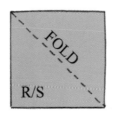

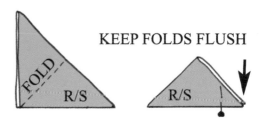

Baste the raw edges of the triangle using
the longest machine stitch; keep the stitching within the 1 cm (³/₈″) seam.

Start basting at the end of the 'two fold' side (by pin) and sew towards the single fold (other end).
Basting the raw edges together prevents movement and keeps the folds aligned.

*Insert the sewing machine needle into the end of the 'two-fold' side before lowering
presser foot. As the presser foot is lowered sometimes the layers slide, but if you
lower the needle first into the fabric it will anchor the layers, holding them firmly.
Now lower presser foot. It is advisable to begin the basting a short distance away
from the folded points, then the feed dogs will pull fabric through more easily
because the presser foot is sitting completely on the fabric.*

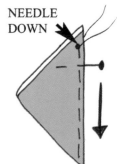

NEEDLE DOWN

2 Make <u>three</u> more using the remaining **Green** squares.

*Remember to 'chain' piece - sew off the first
piece on to the second piece etc.. Cut the
threads afterwards.*

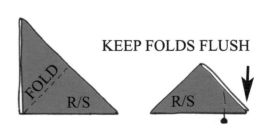

3 Repeat Stage 1 with the four **Red**
14.5 cm (**5¾″**) squares making <u>four</u> more
basted and folded triangles.

33

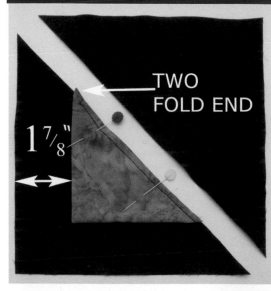

4 Cut all four **Black** 18.5 cm (7¼") squares in half diagonally, forming eight triangles.

5 Take one **Black** triangle - R/S up. Place one **Green** triangle on top. Position the triangle carefully so that the two-fold side is 4.6 cm (1⁷/₈") from left-hand edge of **Black** square; the other side (where there is a single fold) will be approximately 3.25 cm (1³/₈") from the lower/bottom side of the **Black** triangle.

The raw basted edge of the Green triangle is exactly aligned with the raw diagonal edge of the Black section.

Check the 4.6 cm (1⁷/₈") measurement **accurately** before pinning the **Green** triangle in place.

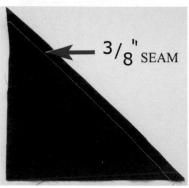

6 Take a second **Black** triangle, place on top (R/S together) and align the raw edges). Pin the layers.

7 Remember to return the stitch length to the regular size before sewing the diagonal side (bias) of triangle using the 1 cm (³/₈") S/A. Try not to stretch the bias edge as you stitch.

8 Remove the basting from the inserted **Green** triangle. Press the seam open and flat.

Remember to take care when pressing any diagonally (bias) cut edge.

9 Turn to R/S and open the **Green** insert. Flatten the insert to form a kite shape. Pin both sides of the kite shape.

Make three more squares the same.

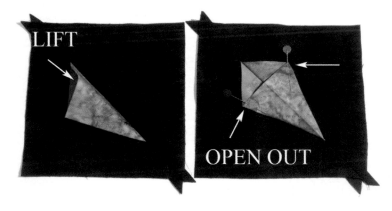

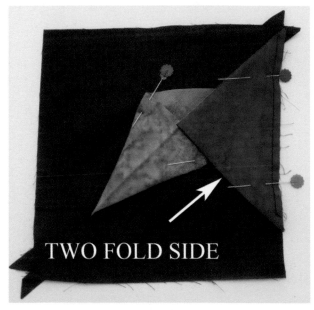

10 Place one **Red** triangle on a **Black** square: The tip of the **Red** triangle is exactly at the top of the **Black** square. The two-folded side is positioned facing away from the centre as indicated by the arrow. The single fold lies alongside the diagonal seam. Align the raw edges of the **Red** triangle with raw edge of **Black** square. Pin in place. For those who like 'belt and braces' (suspenders in USA) and wish to prevent any movement of the pieces, then baste the shape in place as well as pinning.

11 Lay the right-hand square on top R/S together. Match the raw edges. Sew 1 cm ($^3/_8$") seam.

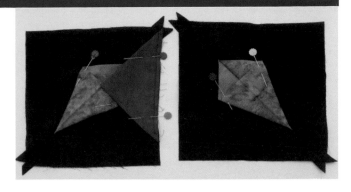

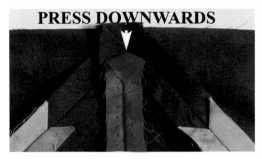

PRESS DOWNWARDS

12 Open out, remove any basting and press the seams open and flat.

On the W/S, press the tip of the inserted **Red** triangle downwards. This action will help when sewing the block together as you can see where the tip of the **Red** shape occurs in the seam - with luck it should be possible to avoid a really big button. Trim the 'ears' from seam.

13 Turn to the R/S, open the inserted **Red** triangle and flatten. Pin the corners.

14 Make another section exactly the same. Don't panic - two **Red** triangles will remain.

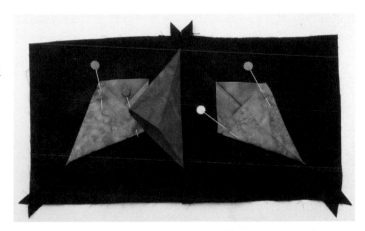

15 Place one of the remaining **Red** triangles on the right. Align the raw edges with the **Black** section. Make sure that the two-fold side faces away from the centre. Pin in place.

*This Red triangle will touch the tip of the previously inserted Red triangle at **A** (where the tip of the previously inserted Red triangle vanishes into the seam).*

16 Place the last **Red** triangle on the left-hand side. BE REALLY CAREFUL to make sure that the two-fold side faces away from the centre. Pin in place. Align the raw edges.

The last Red triangle must overlap the right-hand Red triangle at A. Look closely at the picture to see the positioning.

17 Baste both **Red** triangles in place. Try to get the basting to pass through the junction where the pieces overlap.

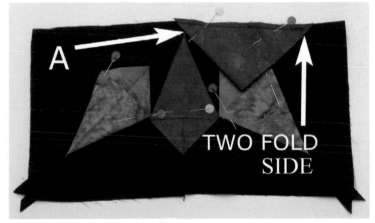

A TWO FOLD SIDE

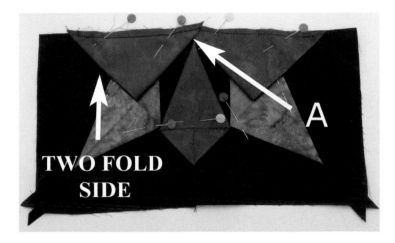

TWO FOLD SIDE A

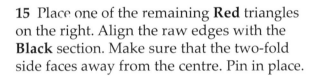

Start the basting near the centre where the points overlap. If you begin at one end, the layers may have shifted by the time you reach that overlapped junction. Therefore the pieces won't line up and... a bigger button might be required!

18 Lay the other half of the block on top. Match the points of the **Red** triangles precisely. Sew the seam through the junction of all these points.

The seam allowance should be 1 cm (³/₈"), BUT deviate if necessary to make very certain that the stitching goes exactly past the end of the Red triangle that is visible in the seam. Have faith - cross fingers - don't give up.

19 Press the seams open and flat.

20 Turn to R/S. Arrange the **Red** triangles in the same manner as the **Green** ones. Pin in place. With luck all the shapes should touch on the corners although a bit of persuasion might be required! If they don't beads, or dare I say buttons, would fill the gaps.

21 Secure corners of the **Red** and **Green** shapes with a small stitch either by hand or machine. And... Lo and Behold... there is a little pocket!

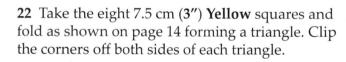

22 Take the eight 7.5 cm (**3"**) **Yellow** squares and fold as shown on page 14 forming a triangle. Clip the corners off both sides of each triangle.

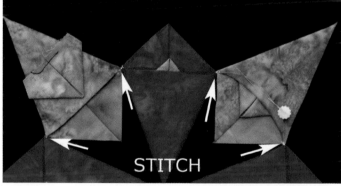

23 Insert one of these triangles into each **Red** and **Green** pocket. The tip of the **Yellow** triangle should be approximately 2.5 cm (**1"**) from the tip of the **Red** or **Green** shape.

24 Once the **Yellow** triangle has been inserted, roll back the pocket edge of the **Red** and **Green** shapes. Sew the rolled edge in place either by hand or machine. Stitch through all the layers. Why not use one of the appliqué stitches as suggested on page 8 or whatever other stitch you fancy?

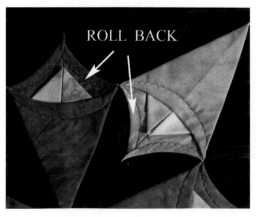

25 Finally, roll the remaining two edges of the **Red** and **Green** sections. Sew in place. Stitch through all the layers.

Aaah... but what if there the points of the **Red** triangles don't meet in the middle? Why not cover the discrepancy with a button/some beads or embroidery, or even a Suffolk Puff?

Suffolk Puff

Sometimes referred to as a Yo-Yo, this particular form of patchwork can be greeted by hoots of derisive laughter, but it can be most effective as a textural embellishment and should not be mocked. Once applied to the centre of your Trumpet Cracker, it creates a dynamic focal point thus emphasising the optical vitality of your completed masterpiece. (What a load of waffle, but you could always offer this explanation if anybody dares to suggest that the addition of a Suffolk Puff conceals your inability to get the central points together.)

The Suffolk Puff is a gathered circle of fabric. Cut one 9 cm (3½") diameter circle. Turn the raw edge over 0.75 cm (¼") approximately to W/S. Sew round with small running stitches. Use a strong thread or double thickness. Once sewn, pull up the thread firmly. Tweak gently to form a pleasing gathered circle before finishing off.

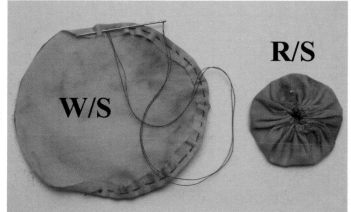

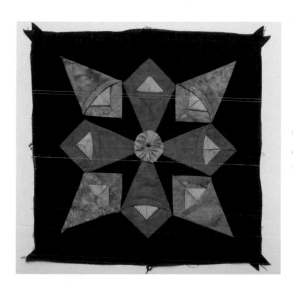

Once completed, couch the Puff in place. Stitch securely especially if the end product will be subject to heavy wear or investigation by inquisitive fingers.

PlayTime

Why not embellish with beads, sequins or buttons stitched to the junctions between the shapes?

How about padding the pockets before rolling back the folded edge and inserting the folded square?

Add a little embroidery in relevant places.

Experiment with manipulating the inserted sections in different ways. They are extremely versatile so have a play. How about remaking the block and turn all or some of the inserted sections round the other way so that the two fold side faces another direction? The end result looks very different.

Try the design in striped fabric for a really zany creation! Why not explore the possibility of an even more twiddlable design? Read on…

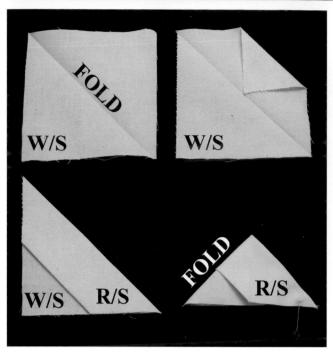

Adding an extra twiddle

For this alternative Trumpet Cracker design, select plain coloured/hand-dyes/batiks or any material that has no discernible right or wrong side, because the W/S is going to show once the folding is complete.

1 Carefully press one of the 14.5 cm (5¾") squares (Stage 1, page 33) in half diagonally.

2 With the W/S up, fold one corner to touch the centre crease. Fold again on the pressed crease to form a triangle. Fold this triangle diagonally in half making a smaller triangle.

3 Baste the raw edge. Repeat with all remaining 14.5 cm (5¾") squares.

4 Follow Stages 4 - 20, pages 34 - 36.

5 Lift up each inserted triangle and roll the centre fold back - bit like turning back a collar.

Continue with rolling the folds and stitching down as described on page 36. Add the little inserts or not - the choice is yours.

Why not make the design in calico (unbleached cotton material) or muslin as it is called in the USA?

Detail: Calico/Muslin Headboard
Jennie Rayment
See page 4

Trumpet Cracker Tote

45 cm (**18"**) square

Short of time? Aren't we all? Here is a very simple tote to construct. For those who ponder on the meaning of words - the definition from Wikipedia is:

"The term tote, meaning "to carry", can be traced back to the 17th century but was not used to describe bags until 1900. Generally a tote holds diverse objects of modest value, its contents varying day-to-day: portable umbrellas, books, towels, stadium/picnic blankets, and other recreational gear; perhaps beverages, finger foods, spare clothes, makeup/dopp kits, and child-care items - all piled atop a set of keys, a cell phone, perhaps a wallet or change purse."

In essence a tote will hold just about anything, although I have to confess I am not sure what a 'dopp kit' is? You, dear reader, can look that word up - I am going to sew instead and create this tote using 'Earthlight' designed by Yolanda Fundora for Blank Quilting (www.urbanamish.com).

Materials
One completed Trumpet Cracker block pages 33 - 36
Two 9 x 115 cm (**3½ x 44"**) strips
One 47 cm (**18½"**) square - tote back
One 47 x 89 cm (**18½ x 35"**) strip - tote lining
90 cm (**36"**) thick tape or webbing
Two 50 cm (**20"**) squares wadding

1 Border the Trumpet Cracker block with the two 9 x 115 cm (**3½ x 44"**) strips. Sew the border strips on with a 0.75 cm (¼") S/A. Add a strip to opposite sides first then add one to the top and the bottom. This is a simple way to attach a border (for more border techniques see page 10). Press the seams open and flat.

2 Lay the bordered panel on a 50 cm (**20"**) square of wadding. Pin in place. Press gently.

Pressing the fabric onto wadding helps to bond both layers lightly together and they are less likely to creep apart as you sew. Do not iron excessively as the wadding may melt: this is particularly important if you are using a polyester based product.

3 Embellish the border with one or two or more lines of stitch parallel to the edge of the Trumpet Cracker block. Align the left-hand edge of the presser foot with the seam around the Trumpet Cracker block, increase the stitch length slightly and sew approximately 0.75 cm (¼") from the seam.

4 Set the zigzag stitch to maximum length and width; sew round the outside edge of the panel to anchor both layers together. Trim the wadding back to the fabric edge.

5 Pin the tote back square to the other piece of wadding. Sew round the edge with maximum length and width zigzag stitch. Trim any excess wadding back to the fabric edge.

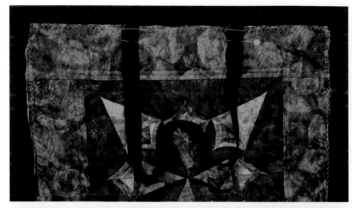

6 To make the handles, cut the 90 cm (**36"**) length of tape or webbing in half to make two handles. Divide one side of the tote panel front into approximate thirds. Position one end of the handle at one third and the other end at two-thirds. Pin in place, then sew the handle on firmly. Keep the stitching within 1 cm ($^3/_8$") from the outer edge. Repeat on the tote back using the remaining length of tape or webbing.

7 Join both sections together to form a larger panel as shown in the photograph. Use 1 cm ($^3/_8$") S/A.

Beware! Stitch the correct sides together - you don't want the handles dangling from the wrong edge.

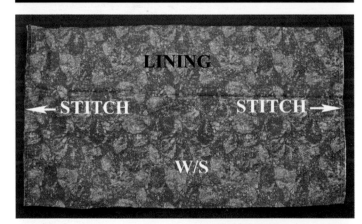

8 Lay the lining on top of the tote panel, R/S together. Pin the layers together along the short sides (by handles). Sew these sides. The tote panel will buckle slightly as the lining section is not the same measurement. Do not panic!

If the lining is cut slightly shorter in length than the overall length of the joined front and back sections of the tote, this will ensure that the lining lies neatly inside the tote on completion.

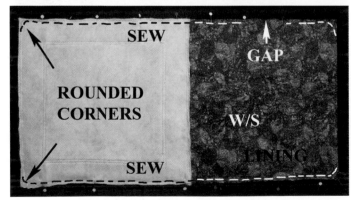

9 Open out the lining and the tote panel. Keeping the two layers R/S together, bring the tote front and back panels together, matching the raw edges. The lining is folded in half. Pin all the layers carefully.

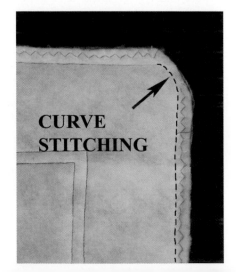

CURVE STITCHING

Use 1 cm ($^3/_8$") S/A and sew along one long side completely, but on the other (opposite) side leave a small gap in the stitching just big enough to turn the bag through. Curve the stitching slightly at the base of each seam. Gently rounded corners on a bag are pleasing.

10 Trim any excess wadding and fabric from the rounded corners. Turn the tote R/S out through the gap. Ease out all the corners with your hand.

11 Sew the gap in the side of the lining either by hand or machine before tucking the lining neatly inside the tote panel.

12 Stitch round the top of the tote to retain the lining and make a decorative finish to the edge.

That is it!

Bingo!!

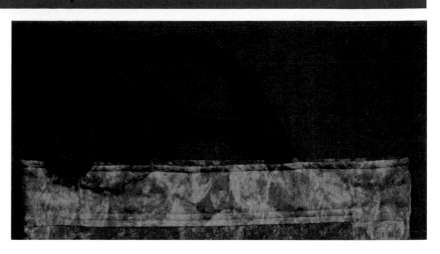

Nine Patch: 122 cm (48")
Lindsey Smith
Top: Starburst, Fizgig, Girandole. Centre: Trumpet Cracker, Roman Candle, Catherine Wheel.
Bottom: Twinkling Star, Skyrocket, Jumping Jack.

More Travel Tips

Do not dry your undies by leaving them draped artistically over the bedside lampshade. If the fabric accidentally touches the bulb, the undies melt, the smell is dire and you are left knickerless. Also, if you have hard boiled eggs in the hotel kettle, do not leave the shelled eggs in the washbasin cooling with the cold tap gently running while you leave the room to pack the car. A peeled hard boiled egg makes an excellent plug. Valuable time is wasted in mopping up the bathroom floor and having to explain to the hotel manager why you had a flood in your room and why the towels are totally sodden.

Froffy Coffee:
170 x 140 cm (70 x 55")
Ann Seed
Features all twelve blocks from this book with bias sashing and corner squares. Enhanced by a manipulated tucked border also with corner squares.

Folded Fancies
138 x 214 cm
(84 x 54")
Lin Barratt
Features all twelve blocks from this book with bias sashing and corner squares plus an extra border constructed from sections of the Whirlygig design.

Twinkling Star

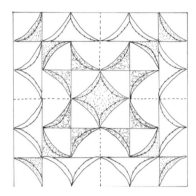

31.5 cm (**12½″**) including outer S/A

Cut

Twelve 6.5 cm (**2½″**) squares - **Purple**
Four 6.5 cm (**2½″**) squares - **Green**
Eight 6.5 x 11.5 cm (**2½″ x 4½″**) strips - **Orange**
Eight 6.5 cm (**2½″**) squares - **Yellow**
Thirty-two 6.5 cm (**2½″**) squares - **Black**
(Lots of little squares to cut - sorry!)

Start Stitching

Seam Allowance 0.75 cm (**¼″**)

1 Press one **Purple** 6.5 cm (**2½″**) square in half diagonally forming a triangle, R/S out.

2 Baste the pressed **Purple** triangle on to one **Green** 6.5 cm (**2½″**) square R/S up; keep the basting within the 0.75 cm (**¼″**) S/A.

3 Repeat last two stages and make three more squares. Sew them together to form a square. Press the seams open and flat.

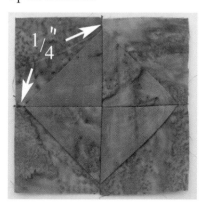

Ensure that there is a 0.75 cm (¼″) gap at the four corners of the Purple central square. If not, unpick the end of the seam and re-stitch.

The next couple of instructions are boring - more apologies...

4 Repeat Stages 1 and 2 with eight **Yellow** 6.5 cm (**2½″**) squares pressed diagonally, R/S out and basted to R/S of the **Black** 6.5 cm (**2½″**) squares.

5 Repeat Stages 1 and 2 with remaining four **Purple** 6.5 cm (**2½″**) squares pressed diagonally, R/S out and basted to R/S of **Black** 6.5 cm (**2½″**) squares.

The design gets more interesting over the page...

6 Arrange all the squares as shown.

7 Sew the squares into strips. Sew the two side sections together first then sew all the top and bottom sections into a row.

Sew the sections together carefully - it is very easy to get them in the wrong order. Nobody likes unpicking stitches!

Match the Yellow triangles very carefully. In the completed and pressed open seam there should be a Yellow 'V'. If you sew exactly along the base of the 'V' shape the points of the triangles on the R/S should be accurate. Deviating in the 0.75 cm (¼") seam allowance is permitted to achieve this goal.

Press all seams open and flat. Trim off the 'ears' from the seams where necessary.

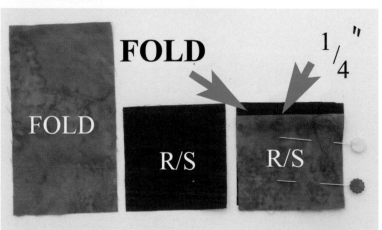

8 Fold one **Orange** 6.5 cm x 11.5 cm (2½" x 4½") strip in half as shown, R/S out. Place onto one **Black** 6.5 cm (2½") square. Pin in place.

Make certain that there is a 0.75 cm (¼") gap between the folded edge of the Orange strip and the edge of the Black square. Wiggle the strip into the correct position if required.

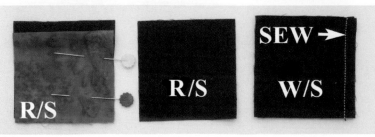

9 Lay another **Black** square on top, sandwiching the rectangle. R/S of Black square to R/S of rectangle. Sew all three sections together where shown.

10 Press the seam open and flat. Turn to R/S. Lift inserted **Orange** strip and arrange as a triangle.

Be picky and persuade the points of the triangle to bisect the corners of the Black squares.

Pin the corners in place and baste the raw edge.

11 Lay out all the pieces, preferably in the same order as the picture!

12 Sew the side sections together to form a strip. Attach these to the centre panel.

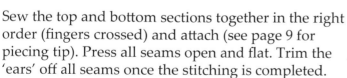

Sew the top and bottom sections together in the right order (fingers crossed) and attach (see page 9 for piecing tip). Press all seams open and flat. Trim the 'ears' off all seams once the stitching is completed.

The completed block should measure 31.5 cm (12½")
square. Trimming the edges is not a good idea as
you may cut the points off the shapes. If there is a
big discrepancy in the measurements then your seam
allowance or cutting out may be a little awry. Be
prepared to stretch the block or ease the edges when
you sew it to another one supposedly the same size,
or alternatively make another! I suggest the former,
as you don't want to do this again!

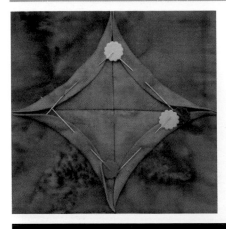

13 Roll back the folded edges of the **Purple** triangles in the centre. Pin in place.

14 Roll back the folded edges of the **Yellow** and remaining **Purple** triangles, pin in place.

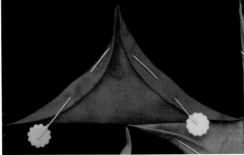

And... you can roll back the edges of the **Orange** triangles as well.

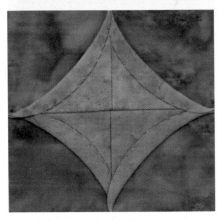

15 Sew the rolled edges in place. See page 8 for stitch suggestions.

On the other hand just catch the rolled edge down with one or two small stitches and put a few beads on top. For those who love hand-stitching, this is an ideal piece to sit and sew in front of the television. Take care not to get carried away by the programme as you may stick the needle in your finger and bleed all over the fabric.

If this happens - spit on the blooded parts and rub the blood away with a clean hanky or tissue. A decent amount of spit is required - not a wussy blob but a generous splodge. Only your spit removes your blood - it's to do with enzymes apparently so don't offer to remove another person's blood as you may expectorate vast quantities and nothing will happen. (I do like the word 'expectorate' and I also like profligate so watch out for that word too!)

Play Time

Why not alter the arrangement of the pieces?

Quite different designs can be made by re-arranging the pieces. Have a go and see what else you can design - here are two more arrangements.

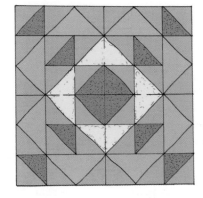

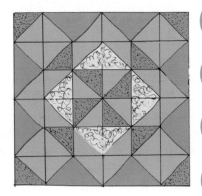

Eight Pointed Star Cushion

40 cm (**16"**) square

Brighten up a chair with this quickly made cushion cover.

Instead of making the entire Twinkling Star - why not just make up the central section using larger sized squares and altering the colour placement?

Materials
Eight 9 cm (**3½"**) squares - **Yellow**
Eight 9 cm (**3½"**) squares - **Green**
Sixteen 9 cm (**3½"**) squares - **Cream**
Four 36.5 x 6.5 cm (**14½ x 2½"**) strips - **Green**
Two 115 x 4 cm (**44 x 1½"**) strips - **Yellow**
One 35.5 cm (**16½"**) square - wadding/batting
One 35.5 cm (**16½"**) square - backing fabric
150 cm (**60"**) piping cord

1 Follow Stages 1 - 8 pages 43 - 44 using the **Yellow/Green** and **Cream** 9 cm (**3½"**) squares.

2 Follow Pinwheel/Partial Seaming Border, page 11 and add a border using the four **Green** 36.5 x 6.5 cm (**14½ x 2½"**) strips.

3 Roll back all the folded edges. Stitch in place as Stage 16 page 46. Mount the completed panel onto the 35.5 cm (**16½"**) square of wadding.

Stitch round the outline of the design and also round the edge of the centre panel of the Green border.

Sew round the outside edge using the longest zigzag stitch to anchor the top fabric to the wadding.

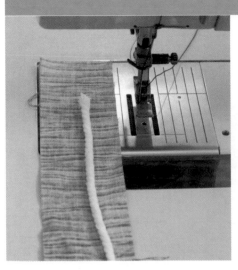

Piping the cushion

1 Join both **Yellow** 115 cm (**44 x 1½"**) strips together, making a longer strip. Join with a straight seam, trim any excess fabric and open the seam out, and press flat.

If you bought an inexpensive piping cord, it should be washed to prevent shrinkage; the better quality cords usually only shrink a little and need not be washed if you follow the method below.

2 Put the zipper foot on the machine setting the needle on your left, i.e. away from the body of the machine.

Bernina users, remember to move the needle position to the extreme left before pressing the foot pedal!

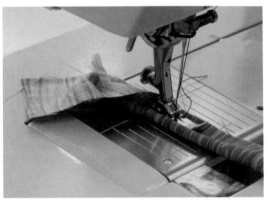

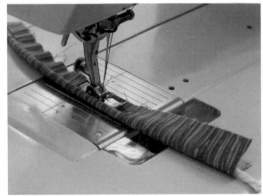

Lay the cord on the wrong side of the strip, setting the start of the cord down by 4 cm (1½"). Fold the fabric over, lining up the edges.

3 Set a long stitch length for speed. Commence sewing 2.5 cm (**1"**) below the start of the cord leaving a short length of fabric un-sewn. Place the finger of your left hand alongside the cord and hold the edges of the fabric together with the right hand; there is no necessity to pin. Sew to the end of the fabric and cord.

4 Place the start of the piping in the centre of any side, aligning the raw edges of the folded strip with the edge of the **Green** fabric.

5 Start stitching at the same place as in Stage 3 leaving a short length of fabric unattached. Sew clockwise round the work, matching the edges of the piping to the edges of the cushion.

Stop sewing approximately 7 cm (**3"**) from the first corner, clip the fabric carefully and curve the cord in a gentle arc round the corner. Draw a curve on each corner to get all the arcs the same.

A lid/small saucer/large mug makes an ideal template. Failing to have gently arced corners results in pointed 'ears' to the finished cushion. (Who wants pointy ears?)

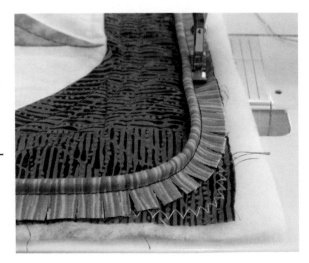

Do be careful when you clip through the edge of the piping fabric that you don't cut the cord as well.

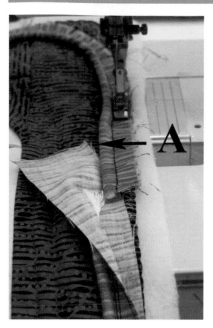

6 Sew round all the corners with the edge of the piping fabric aligned with the drawn curve.

7 Stop stitching about 7 cm (**3"**) from the end of the cord. At **A,** fold the raw edge over 0.75 cm (**¼"**).

Trim the other end of the piping, butting it up exactly to the start of the cord.

8 Fold the excess fabric over this join and sew past.

Butting the ends of the cord together under two layers of fabric will help to conceal any shrinkage in the cord when the cushion is washed. (You can tell if your friends wash their cushions as you can often feel a small gap between the cord ends in the piping join.)

9 Lay the 35.5 cm (**16½"**) square of backing R/S down on to the cushion front. Pin in place. Continue to use the zipper foot and sew round the outside of the piping.

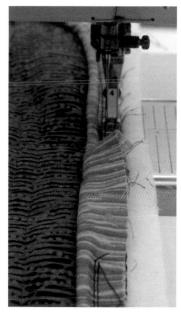

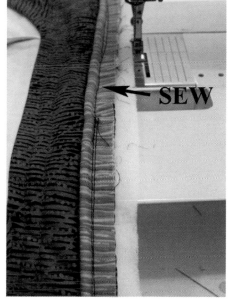

Push the piping cord firmly up to the presser foot edge with your left hand. Try to get the presser foot edge as close as possible to the piping cord. This will ensure that the cord fits snugly round the edge of the completed cushion cover.

10 Leave a large gap on one side unsewn to turn the cover through and insert the cushion pad.

11 Trim any excess fabric and wadding from the corners. Turn the cover R/S out through the gap and insert the pad. Stitch the gap together by hand - a little difficult to do on the machine!

12 Thump the completed cushion well to drive the corners of the pad into the corners of the cover - this also gets rid of all your frustrations! Place the beautiful cushion on a sofa or chair, sit back and relax!

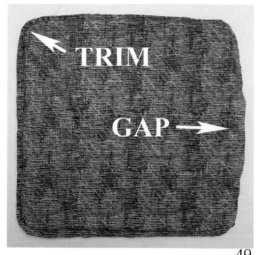

Collection of Colourful Creations: Shelagh Jarvis
Nine patch lap quilt, plus a tote bag featuring the 'Twinkling Star' in
two different colour ways. All created and designed by Shelagh Jarvis

Fizgig

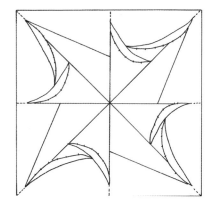

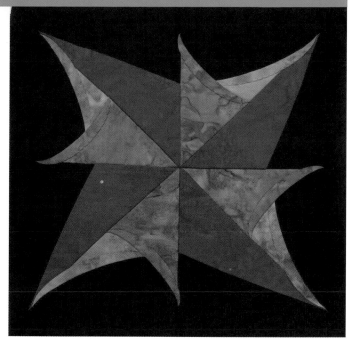

31.5 cm (**12½″**) including outer S/A

Cut

Four 17.5 cm (**6 ⁷/₈″**) squares - **Black** (*Cut each square in half diagonally, making two triangles*)
Two 15 cm (**6″**) squares - **Green** (*Cut each square in half diagonally, making two triangles*)
Two 15 cm (**6″**) squares - **Red** (*Cut each square in half diagonally, making two triangles*)
Two 15 cm (**6″**) squares - **Yellow** (*Cut each square in half diagonally, making two triangles*)

Start Stitching
Seam Allowance 0.75 cm (¼″)

Look at the photographs carefully - watch the direction of the fold on the Red and Yellow triangles.

1 With the W/S facing up, fold one **Red** triangle in half. Fold in half from the tip of the triangle at **A** to the centre of one side at **B**. This forms a different shaped triangle with R/S out. Press the folded triangle.

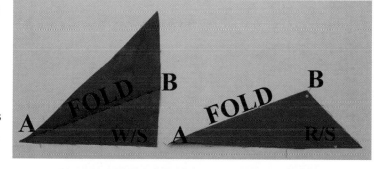

2 Lay this folded triangle onto the R/S of one **Black** triangle. Align the long edge of the **Red** triangle with the long (bias) edge of the **Black** one. Pin in place. Baste round the raw edges. Keep the basting within the S/A.

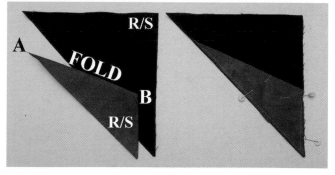

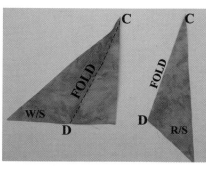

3 Repeat with one **Yellow** triangle. Lay the triangle W/S up as shown in the photograph and fold from **C** to **D.**

This forms another triangle which is a <u>mirror</u> image of the folded **Red** one.

Look closely - I had to do it twice as well!

Place the **Yellow** triangle onto the R/S of another **Black** one. Align raw edges. Pin and baste in place.

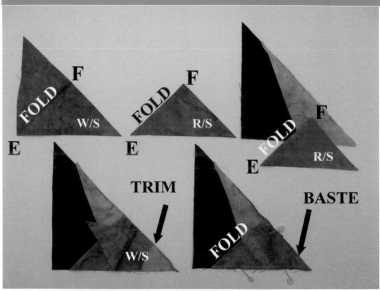

4 Fold one **Green** triangle in half (R/S outside) from **E** to **F**. Place this smaller triangle onto the R/S of a **Yellow** and **Black** triangle.

Align the raw edges. Trim the underside of the **Green** triangle. Pin in place. Baste the raw edges.

5 Take one **Yellow** and **Green** and one **Red** triangle and sew together to form a square. Press the seam open and flat.

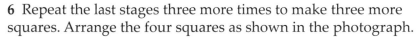

6 Repeat the last stages three more times to make three more squares. Arrange the four squares as shown in the photograph.

7 Stitch two squares together to make one half of the block. Repeat with the other two to form the other half. Press the seam open and flat.

8 Trim the ears from the seams before sewing the two halves together. Match the points of the **Red** and **Green** triangles at the centre.

Look carefully at the colours in the seam - there is a **Red** and **Green** 'V' at the top of the seam. Sew exactly past the point of the 'V'. With luck and a following wind, this should ensure accurate points to the **Red** and **Green** triangles on the R/S.

9 Press the seam flat and open. It is bulky, so give it a good flattening!

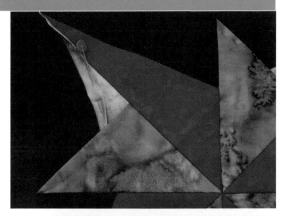

10 Roll back the edge of the **Yellow** triangles and sew in place by hand or machine (page 8).

11 Roll back the edge of the **Green** triangle and sew in place.

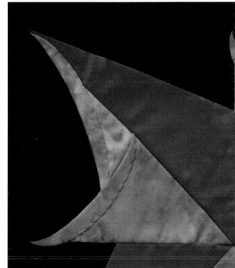

That is it - easy wasn't it?

Play Time

Add a few inserts for a subtly different appearance to the Fizgig block. Cut four 8 cm (**3"**) squares. Fold into triangles (Stages 10 - 11, page 14).

Tuck one into the pocket beneath one of the folded triangles.

Roll back the edge of the triangle and stitch the folded edge in place.

Read on for more ideas...

More Play Time

Consider arranging the four squares in a different format before sewing them together to make the block.

What about ignoring the **Green** triangles and just playing with the **Red** and **Yellow** ones? If all the **Red** and **Yellow** triangles were kept the same size as in the original Fizgig design but were all identically pressed and folded the same i.e. no mirror images, could the design be sewn together? No. Why? The **Yellow** triangles are too long and won't fit in the seams.

Ha! Rectify this problem by cutting the **Yellow** sections smaller. Cut two 12 cm (4¾″) squares and divide diagonally in two. Fold the four triangles as per the **Red** ones - these smaller triangles will fit in the seam.

But… What if all the **Red** and **Yellow** triangles were the same size?

Fizgig Whirl

1 Cut two 12 cm (4¾″) squares in **Red** and **Yellow** and four 17.5 cm (6⅞″) **Black** squares. Divide all the squares diagonally making two triangles.

2 Fold all the **Red** and **Yellow** triangles as shown in Stage 1, page 51. Baste each one to a **Black** triangle.

3 Make up the block as described on pages 51 - 52.

4 Roll back the folded edges of the **Yellow** and **Red** triangles and sew in place.

There you are - a Fizgig Whirl and if the points don't meet in the centre - a button perhaps?

Quags, Quillows and Secret Pillows

To explain, a quillow and a secret pillow are one and the same - a small quilt that folds into a pillow. In case you are confused - pillows in America are called cushions in Great Britain. Supposedly we all speak English, but there are many differences in the vocabulary. This can be most confusing. For instance, tacking (UK term for a long temporary stabilising stitch) is basting in the USA; cross grain (referring to a bias cut) in the UK would mean a cut from selvedge to selvedge to an American. Calico in UK speak (unbleached cotton material) is called muslin in the States. Moving to other common words, bumpers are fenders, bonnets are hoods, taps are faucets and humping doesn't mean the same in the USA as it does in the UK. There are many other variations in our 'common' tongue.

Floradorable Quag quilt: Star block page 47, floral block patterns available on www.jennierayment.com

Now a quag is a 'Jennie' word. What is a quag? It is a quilt that turns into a bag - what else would you call it? (Any other suggestions are not welcome!) A quag is amazingly useful for travelling - you have a bag and a snuggly quilt to wrap round yourself when in a car or on a plane.

Floradorable Quag bag

A Quag is ideal for picnics as you can cart the food and drink in the bag and sit on the quilt. (Consider backing the quilt in plastic then it will be waterproof and you won't get a damp bottom when sitting on the grass.) For mothers and new babies it's a winner. All the baby paraphernalia could be shoved into the bag and then the babe can enjoy rolling on the quilt reveling in the touchy-feely texture.

Mind you, if you made the bag panel larger, there might be room to stuff the baby in as well - no need push a stroller or pram just carry the quag!

To make a quag you need a quilt and a separate panel. Both the quilt and the panel have a handle stitched into the binding. The quilt is folded in a certain fashion so that it will fit into the panel. The panel should measure one third of the width and length of the quilt or thereabouts. Don't be so fussy and work to a micro measurement - a fraction more or less between the related sizes of the panel and the quilt won't ruin the finished project.

Fizgig Quag bag

Fizgig Quag

Four Fizgig, four Girandole and one Roman Candle completed blocks were chosen for the quilt part of this quag. These designs were sewn together with extra strips inserted between each block to create a larger panel. Three different coloured borders were also attached. Here are brief instructions on making this quag.

Materials

Nine 31 cm (**12½″**) squares
50 x 115 cm (**20 x 44″**) strip **Cream**
50 x 115 cm (**20 x 44″**) strip **Black**
50 x 115 cm (**20 x 44″**) strip **Green**
50 x 115 (**20 x 44″**) strip **Red**
140 cm (**56″**) square wadding/batting - Quilt
140 cm (**56″**) square backing fabric - Quilt
50 cm (**20″**) square wadding/batting - Panel
50 cm (**20″**) square wadding/batting - Panel

Quag Quilt 132 x 132 cm (**54 x 54″**)

Seam Allowance 0.75 cm (**¼″**)

1 From the **Cream** fabric cut twelve 6.5 x 31 cm (**2½ x 12½″**) strips. In addition, cut four 6.5 cm (**2½″**) **Green** squares.

Lay these strips and squares between the previously made blocks. Sew all the pieces together to form a large square panel.

2 Measure the sides of the panel and cut four 6.5 cm (**2½″**) wide **Cream** strips to this measurement plus four 6.5 cm (**2½″**) **Green** squares. Attach these pieces to the sides of the panel.

3 Add the borders. Three borders were used on this quag but the selected widths can be adjusted if desired. Measure the sides and cut each individual border strip the correct length.

First border: Cut 5 cm (**2″**) wide **Green** strips. Second border: Cut 3.5 cm (**1¼″**) wide **Red** strips. Third border: Cut 8 cm (**3¼″**) wide **Black** strips. Stitch these to the centre panel to form the completed quilt top.

4 Press well. Lay the quilt top on the 140 x 140 cm (**56 x 56″**) square of wadding and backing fabric. Sandwich the three layers. Pin/baste/Tak gun* all the layers firmly before quilting by hand or machine. Alternatively, anchor the layers with a few stitches, buttons or beads sewn through all three materials at various intervals. Sew round the outside edge of the quilt to anchor all three layers together in preparation for binding.

*(*Tak or tack gun: Gadget that fires small plastic tags through all the fabrics and anchors the materials tightly together)*

Quag Panel

44.5 x 44.5 cm (**18 x 18"**)

1 Make one Girandole 31 cm (**12½"**) square (page 75).

2 Add borders. First border: Cut 4 cm (**1½"**) **Green** strips. Second Border: Measure the sides of the panel and cut four 6.5 cm (**2½"**) wide **Red** strips this measurement. For the corners cut four 6.5 cm (**2½"**) **Green** squares. Sew both borders onto the central square. Press well.

3 Lay the panel on the 50 x 50 cm (**20 x 20"**) square of wadding and backing fabric. Pin/baste/tack the layers together before commencing any quilting. Sew round outside edge to secure all three layers.

Handles

1 Cut two 11 x 50 cm (**4½ x 20"**) **Red** strips.

2 Take one of these strips and press 0.75 cm (**¼"**) to the W/S along one long edge. Press 3.5 cm (**1¼"**) to W/S along the other long edge.

3 Cut a 4.5 x 50 cm (**1¾ x 20"**) strip of wadding/batting. Lay the wadding inside the pressed strip. Fold both sides of the pressed strip over so that they overlap each other in the centre. The wadding is enclosed inside the pressed band. Pin the layers in place.

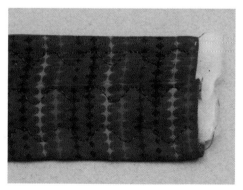

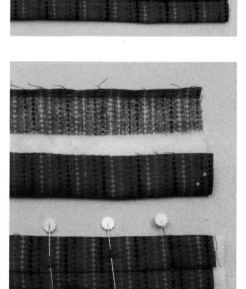

4 Sew along the centre fold first then sew either side.

Experiment with a decorative stitch pattern in a contrasting colour. Try some of those stitches that you have never used on your sewing machine.

5 Repeat Stages 2 - 4 with the remaining 11 x 50 cm (**4½ x 20"**) strip to make a second handle.

6 Pin one handle to the back of the quag panel, W/S of handle to W/S of panel. Space the handle ends at one-third intervals approximately along one side. Align the handle ends with the raw edge of the panel. Sew the handle firmly in place, keeping the stitching close to the raw edge so that it will be hidden by the binding.

7 Bind the raw edge of the panel (page 86). The ends of the handle will be covered by the binding.

8 Attach the other handle to the middle of one side of the quilt. Check that the ends of both handles are positioned at the same distance apart as on the panel. Bind the raw edge of the quilt.

Making up and folding the Quag

This is the best bit!

1 Position the panel in the centre of one side of the quilt. The **R/S** of the panel must face the **W/S** of quilt. The handles lie on the outside edge. Pin both pieces carefully.

2 Sew the panel to the back to the quilt. This can be done by hand or on the machine. If using the machine, use invisible thread/nylon filament in the **bobbin** and **tighten** the top thread tension a little. Tightening the top thread tension prevents the top thread colour showing on the quilt front.

3 Folding time!

Lay the quilt R/S up on a flat surface. Fold one side one third over.

Fold the opposite side one third over.

Fold the bottom (other end from handles) one third up.

Fold the length of the quilt in half.

Turn the entire piece over so that the panel is on the top and thrust hands in between the panel and the back of the quilt.

Grab the corners of the quilt and turn through. Wriggle a bit, probably both you and the quilt! With a bit of pat and a pull the complete quilt will fold into the space between the panel and the back of the quilt. Even more miraculously, the front of the panel is now on the outside.

Grab hold of the handles and admire - the Fizgig and Girandole quilt is now folded neatly inside… a bag!

Voilà… a quag!

P.S. This folding gets easier once you understand the principle.

Now I've made you curse trying to turn the quag right-side out, perhaps you will smile at this little tale?

Having known each other for many years, Fred and Flossie decided that they would like to marry and both being of a careful nature they thought they should discuss all the household arrangements before committing to the marriage ceremony. As they lingered over a pleasant supper in a local restaurant, they chatted over various things like when to do the washing and the housework, when to go shopping and other such domestic details. Fred thought he would just enquire about another matter dear to his heart.

"Flossie", he said "We should discuss bedroom matters - how often do you feel we should engage in intimacy?"

She coyly replied "In-frequently."

"Aaah!" he responded, "Would you consider that to be one word or two?"

Leeks in the Kettle!

No, this is not a spelling mistake - I really do mean leeks as in the vegetable. Why on earth would any one have leeks in a kettle (hot pot in the USA)? Quite simple, they will accompany my salmon for supper.

Staying away from home and constantly being faced with a regime of restaurant/pub grub is a tad wearisome, so I cook in my room instead. Not for me, the lugging of a microwave or other cooking gadget around the world. No, I like to use what is to hand - the kettle. Kettles will remain boiling if you leave the lid off or prop it upright but this can cause a problem as the fire alarm goes off if too much steam is created. Forcing all the guests to leave the hotel unnecessarily is not acceptable behaviour so please be careful. It is also imperative that everything in your room is left in good condition for the next guest - it would be most unfortunate for the next guest to find an odd potato or a boiled egg in the kettle.

Whirlygig Bag: Jennie Rayment

Last year, tired and hungry and choosing to stay in my hotel room, it occurred to me that leeks cook swiftly. Would finely sliced leeks cook in the kettle? If so, they would accompany my salmon and new potatoes (I am a dab hand at spuds in the kettle and salmon will cook if boiling water is poured over a thin fillet and left for a few minutes). Yes, my theory worked - boil the leeks for a couple of minutes, then strain off the excess water. Bingo! Cleaning out of the remaining rings of leek off the electrical element was the only snag, but my toothbrush worked a treat. Once the kettle was rinsed out thoroughly and re-boiled there was no discernible aftertaste nor smell of onions, and my tea tasted fine. Consequently I was delighted.

A few weeks later after this previous experiment, I repeated it. This time after cooking there was a faint onion smell lingering in my room - could I get rid of it? No, I sniffed the inside of the kettle that was fine, I sniffed the carpet/curtains/bed linen - they didn't smell. Where did the faint whiff of old onions come from? On the third day as I was about to depart, it dawned on me - the kettle didn't smell but the lid did! A waft of leeks came faintly from the solid plastic lid - it had absorbed the odour. Each time I boiled the kettle the pong became more obvious as the kettle heated up, but it had never occurred to me to sniff the lid, just the body of the kettle. Not a problem, I just gave the entire underside of the lid a jolly good spray of Chanel No 5 and left the room.

Therefore, should you be in a hotel room in some part of the world, and when you boil the kettle the air is fragrant with Chanel No 5, you will know this is where I cooked my leeks!

Scrappy Zappy Do Bag: Trish Harrocks
Created from part of the design. Tucked inserts as described in Stages 10 - 14 pages 14 - 15. Embellished with beads.

Skyrocket

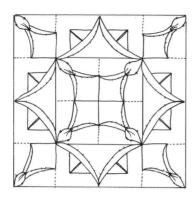

31.5 cm (**12½″**) including outer S/A

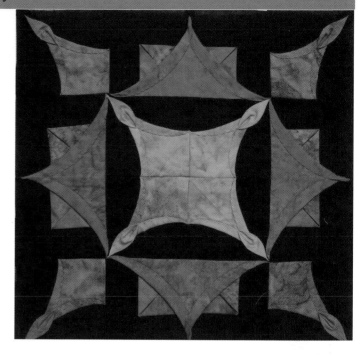

Cut
Four 9 cm (**3½″**) squares - **Yellow**
Four 9 cm (**3½″**) squares - **Purple**
Four 9 x 16.5 cm (**6½ x 3½″**) rectangles - **Orange**
Eight 10 cm (**3⅞″**) squares - **Black** (*Cut each square in half diagonally, making two triangles*)
Eight 7.5 cm (**3″**) squares - **Green**
Eight 9 cm (**3½″**) squares - **Black**

Start Stitching
Seam Allowance 0.75 cm (¼″)

1 Press one **Yellow** 9 cm (**3½″**) square in half diagonally R/S out forming a triangle. Place it onto the R/S of one **Black** triangle as shown. Position the folded edge of the **Yellow** triangle <u>exactly</u> 0.75 cm (¼″) from the left-hand edge of the **Black** triangle.

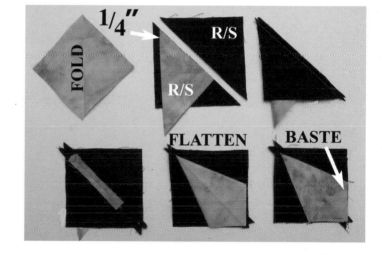

2 Lay another **Black** triangle on top R/S together. Sew the diagonal edge, taking care not to stretch the diagonal (bias) edge. Press the seam open and flat, flattening the top of the **Yellow** triangle, as shown in left-hand photograph.

3 Turn to the R/S and open the inserted **Yellow** triangle. Flatten into a 'kite' shape. Baste the raw edges. Make three more.

4 Arrange these four sections to form the Skyrocket centre. Sew two sections together to form one half - sew the other two sections together to form the other half. Join both halves together, matching the seams in the middle. Trim the 'ears' off the corners. Press the seams open and flat to reduce bulk.

61

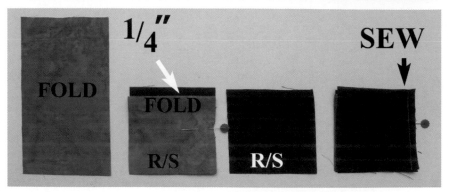

5 Fold one **Orange** 9 x 16.5 cm (3½ x 6½") rectangle in half R/S out. Place it on the R/S of one 9 cm (3½") **Black** square. Ensure that the raw edges of the folded rectangle are aligned with the edges of the **Black** square. The folded edge of rectangle <u>must be positioned 0.75 cm (¼") from the edge of the **Black** square.</u>

Put a pin in one side of the **Orange** rectangle to hold it in place, inserting the pin parallel to the folded edge. Place another **Black** square on top, R/S together. The folded rectangle is now sandwiched between the two **Black** squares. Stitch down the pinned side. If you don't insert the pin as a marker, it is easy to stitch the wrong side and the end result may not be quite what is required!

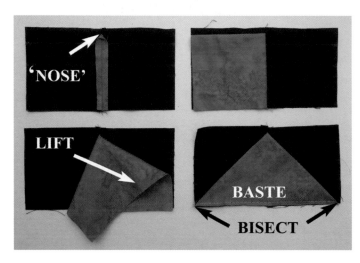

6 Press the seam open and flat. Squash the nose of the **Orange** rectangle downwards onto the **Orange** fabric, not the **Black**.

7 Turn this section to the R/S and lift up the **Orange** rectangle. Open it out and arrange into a triangle.

The points of the Orange triangle should neatly bisect the corners of the Black squares. Jiggle these points into position if necessary.

8 Pin the layers in place and then press. Baste along the raw edge. Make three more using the remaining **Black** squares and **Orange** rectangles.

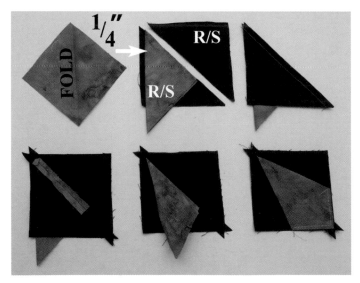

9 Using the four **Purple** 9 cm (3½") squares and all the remaining **Black** triangles, repeat the Stages 1 - 3, page 61.

10 Lay out all the pieces as shown in the picture.

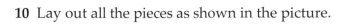

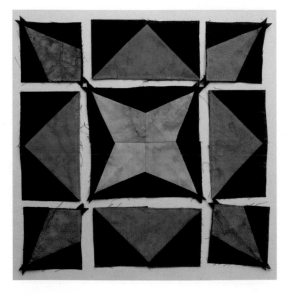

11 Sew the sides onto the centre section first and then join all the top and bottom pieces to form two rows.

12 Attach the top and bottom rows.

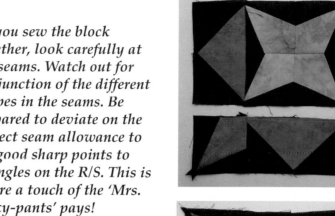

As you sew the block together, look carefully at the seams. Watch out for the junction of the different shapes in the seams. Be prepared to deviate on the correct seam allowance to get good sharp points to triangles on the R/S. This is where a touch of the 'Mrs. Picky-pants' pays!

Trim any ears and press seams open and flat.

13 Fold all eight 7.5 cm (**3"**) **Green** squares into triangles (Stages 10 - 11, page 14).

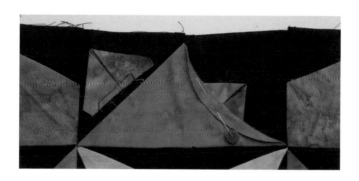

14 Tuck one of these into the pockets at the back of each **Orange** triangle. Roll back the **Orange** folded edge. Sew the folded edge in place using... guess what? The Blind Hem or similar appliqué stitch or even... do it by hand - sewing that is! (See page 8 for advice on stitch techniques.)

Tuck the Green triangle fairly deeply into the pocket otherwise as you sew along the folded Orange edge the base of the triangle will not be caught into the stitching and it may fall out at a later date.

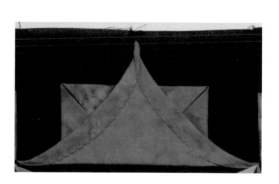

15 Roll back the edges of the **Purple** shapes until they touch each other in the centre of the kite shape. Sew both edges up to this junction. The remaining section (at the tip) can now be opened out to form a small petal. Secure the sides of the petal with a few small stitches.

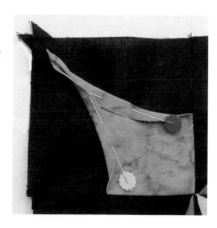

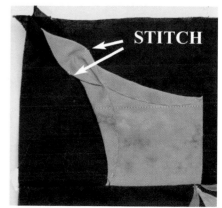

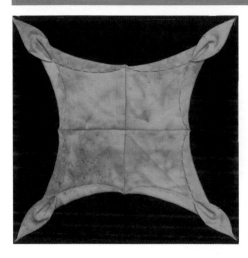

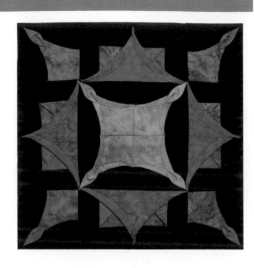

16 Roll the edges of the central sections and sew in place. Once again you can open out the tips of the **Yellow** pieces to form a small petal.

Play Time

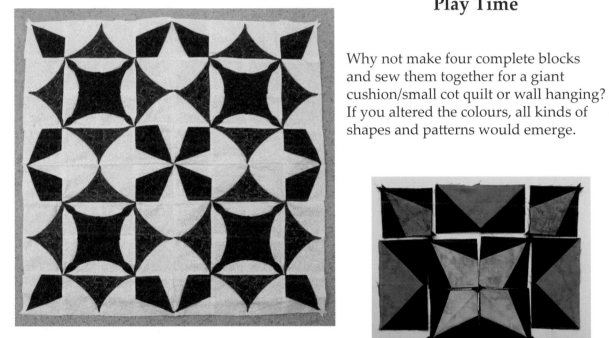

Why not make four complete blocks and sew them together for a giant cushion/small cot quilt or wall hanging? If you altered the colours, all kinds of shapes and patterns would emerge.

What about rearranging the pieces before you sew the block together?

There are several other arrangements of all these pieces - play!

Firecracker

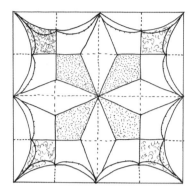

31.5 cm (**12½″**) including outer S/A

Cut
Eight 9 cm (**3½″**) squares - **Orange**
Four 9 cm (**3½″**) squares - **Yellow**
Four 9 cm (**3½″**) squares - **Green**
Eight 10 cm (**3⁷/₈″**) squares - **Black** (*Cut each square in half diagonally, making two triangles*)
Eight 10 cm (**3⁷/₈″**) squares - **Green** (*Cut each square in half diagonally, making two triangles*)

This block is related to Skyrocket (page 61) employing the same construction techniques.

Start Stitching
Seam Allowance 0.75 cm (**¼″**)

1 Follow Stages 1 - 3, page 61 and make four squares using all four 9 cm (**3½″**) **Green** squares and eight **Black** triangles.

2 Follow Stages 1 - 3 page 61 and make four squares using all four 9 cm (**3½″**) **Yellow** squares and the remaining **Black** triangles.

3 Take one **Orange** 9 cm (**3½″**) square (press in half diagonally forming a triangle), one **Black** and one **Green** triangle. Follow Stages 1 - 3, page 61, BUT lay one **Black** triangle R/S down first, add the **Orange** triangle then put the **Green** one on top. Make three more.

4 Reverse the procedure. Lay a **Green** triangle down first then an **Orange** 9 cm (**3½″**) square (pressed in half diagonally forming a triangle); a **Black** triangle is placed on top. Make three more.

5 Sew the centre sections first.

Stitch two sections to form one half of the centre. Repeat with the other two sections.

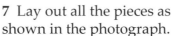

6 Sew the two halves to form the centre panel.

Match the points carefully in the middle of the design, and if they should not quite meet rest assured a button would be a most attractive embellishment to this block!

7 Lay out all the pieces as shown in the photograph.

8 Sew two sections together and attach to both sides of the completed central panel.

Join the four top and bottom sections together to form two rows and sew in place. Press the seams open and flat.

Don't forget to trim the 'ears' as you go. (The fabric ears not yours!)

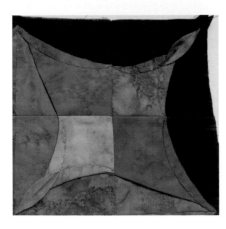

9 Roll back all the folded edges. Stitch the rolled back edges using one of the appliqué stitches (page 8) unless you prefer to sew in place by hand!

(Do you get the impression I am not a fan of hand sewing. In fact, if I am honest my hand stitching is so dire, it resembles a drunken spider cavorting across the fabric in a frenetic fashion.)

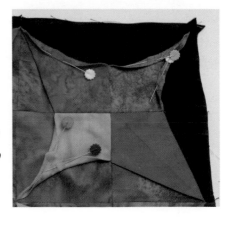

Play Time

Consider arranging the sections in a different pattern.

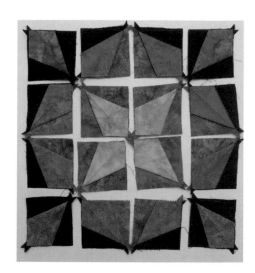

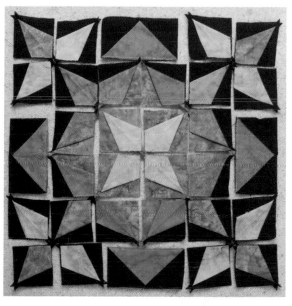

Combine all sixteen squares from the Firecracker block with the twelve sections from the Skyrocket design (page 61) to make a much larger panel. Four more squares are required to complete the design. To create these extra pieces, cut four 9 cm (3½") **Yellow** and four 10 cm (3⁷/₈") **Black** squares and follow (Stages 1 - 3, page 61).

There are many ways to arrange all these pieces, take a few moments and have a play.

In this completed wall-hanging, some edges were left unrolled and additional squares were folded and tucked under the centre **Purple** sections.

Fold eight 7.5 cm (3") squares as described in Stages 10 - 11, page 14 and tuck these shapes under the **Green** triangles and stitch in place. Cut four 5 x 7.5 cm (2 x 3") **Yellow** strips and fold as explained on page 73. Tuck these folded shapes under the centre sections. Sew in place.

Nine Patch:
114 cm (45")
Ann Seed
Top: Trumpet Cracker, Girandole, Starburst.
Centre: Twinkling Star, Roman Candle, Catherine Wheel.
Bottom: Skyrocket, Fizgig, Jumping Jack.

Fizgig and Starburst cushions:
Shelagh Jarvis

Patchwork Coat :
Shelagh Jarvis
Created from Whirlygig design and with bias sashing linking the sections.

Calico Shirt: Jennie Rayment

Roman Candle

31.5 cm (**12½″**) including outer S/A

Cut

Eight 9 cm (**3½″**) squares - **Red**

Four 9 cm (**3½″**) squares - **Yellow**

Four 10 cm (**3⁷⁄₈″**) squares - **Yellow** (*Cut each square in half diagonally, making two triangles*)

Four 9 cm (**3½″**) squares + Four 7 x 16.5 cm (**2¾ x 6½″**) strips - **Black**

Four 4 x 16.5 cm (**1½ x 6½″**) strips - **Orange**

Four 9 cm (**3½″**) squares - **Green**

Four 6.5 cm (**2½″**) squares - **Green**

Four 3.5 x 16.5 cm (**1¼ x 6½″**) strips - **Green**

Four 5 x 7.5 cm (**2 x 3″**) strips - **Purple**

Before beginning Roman Candle, be aware that this is the hardest design in the book. Why? Getting the points of the Red triangles to meet accurately at the centre is a trifle tricky, but remember a button or a few beads are absolutely excellent at providing both a focal point and disguising a little deviation in the seams!

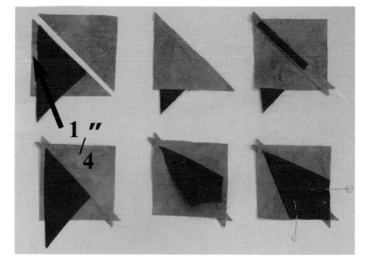

Start Stitching

Seam Allowance 0.75 cm (¼″)

1 Take one **Red** 9 cm (**3½″**) square and two **Yellow** triangles and follow Stages 1 - 3, page 61. (Basting along the raw edge can be omitted - pin the layers in place carefully instead.) Make four.

2 Fold one **Red** 9 cm (**3½″**) square diagonally forming a triangle. Lay this triangle on to one **Red** and **Yellow** square as shown in the photograph, aligning all the raw edges of the triangle with the raw edges of the square. Make sure that the folded side of the triangle touches the tip of the previously inserted **Red** section. Peer closely at the picture to check the alignment of the pieces.

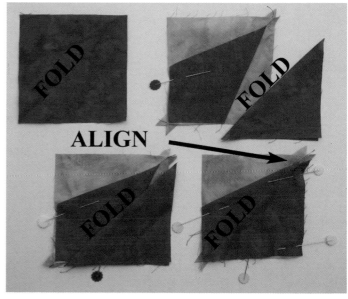

69

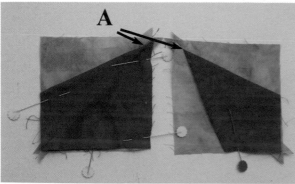

3 Pin the **Red** triangle in place. Take one more **Red** and **Yellow** square. Join the two squares together matching the tips of the previously inserted **Red** sections at **A**.

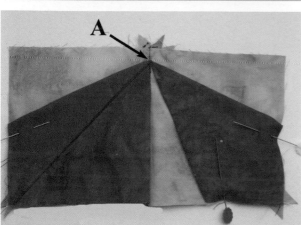

With luck, when you open the piece out, all three tips of all the **Red** sections should meet at **A**. If not, unpick the top section of the seam and re-stitch, or buy a bigger button.

Press the seam open and flat and trim off 'ears'. (It's one of those Van Gogh moments!)

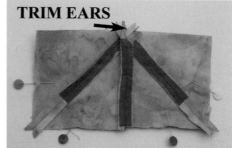

Lift the **Red** triangle up and open out to form a 'kite' shape. Press the shape in place.

4 Repeat the last two stages with the remaining two **Red** and **Yellow** squares.

Both halves of the centre section are now completed and there should be two Red 9 cm (3½″) squares left - do not panic YET!

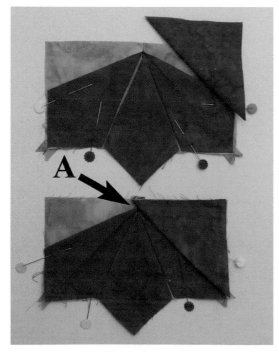

5 Fold one of the remaining **Red** squares diagonally making a triangle. Lay it on the right-hand side. The folded side of the **Red** triangle will touch the tips of the other **Red** sections at **A**. All raw edges should be aligned. Pin the shape in place.

6 Fold the last **Red** square into a triangle and lay it on the left-hand side. Take care that the folded edge of the **Red** triangle touches the tips of the other **Red** sections.

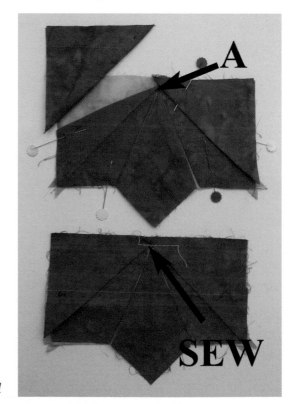

The last **Red** triangle will overlap the preceding one at **A**.

7 Sew across the junction of the last two triangles to keep them exactly in place.

Nearly there - lying down in a darkened room with a cold compress might not be necessary.

8 Join both halves together. Match the points up in the centre.

9 Lift the last **Red** triangles up and open out to form kite shapes. Press in place.

10 Baste round the outside edge to hold all the layers together. Trim the excess fabric from the sides to form a square.

Word of warning - think before you trim - it is just the excess fabric from the Red shape you are trimming and nothing else. You really don't want to have to go through all that fussing about getting the points together kerfuffle again or do you?

11 Relax - the tough bit is over - the rest should be a doddle. Fold one 6.5 cm (2½″) **Green** square diagonally. Lay on to one corner of the centre section. Align all raw edges before basting in place. Trim part of the underside of the **Green** triangle to reduce bulk in the seam. Repeat on the other corners with remaining **Green** squares.

12 Press one 4 x 16.5 cm (1½ x 6½″) **Orange** strip in half lengthways.

13 Follow the photograph below. Put one **Black** 7 x 16.5 cm (2¾ x 6½″) strip on top of one **Green** 3.5 x 16.5 cm (1¼ x 6½″) strip, sandwiching a folded and pressed **Orange** strip in between. Align all the raw edges. Stitch the three pieces together. Press the seams towards the **Green** section.

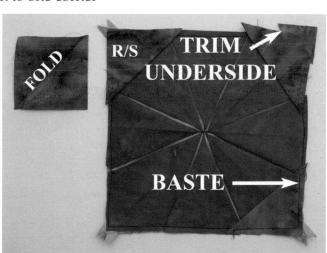

Repeat this stage three more times.

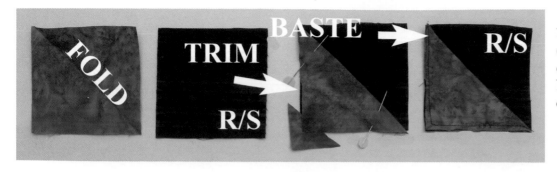

14 Fold one 9 cm (3½") **Green** square diagonally in half. Lay it on the R/S of one **Black** square.

Reduce the bulk in the seams by trimming part of the underside of the **Green** triangle. Baste round the raw edges.

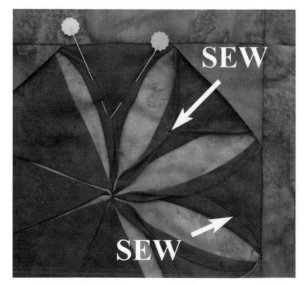

15 The best bit is putting the design together. Arrange the pieces as shown in the picture above.

16 Attach the side sections first. Join the top and bottom sections to form a strip. Sew in place.

Now for a bit of fun! You can roll, fold, twitch and tweak!

17 Roll the sides of the **Red** sections towards the centre so that they meet. Sew these sides together at this junction.

Stitch the rolled back edges in place. Sew up to the junction and down the other side leaving the tip of the shape unstitched.

Have a look at page 8 for advice on various types of machine appliqué stitches that could prove useful.

18 For added extra bit of pzzazz, roll back the edges of the tip of the shape to form a small petal-like shape. Sew the sides of the petal with a few small stitches.

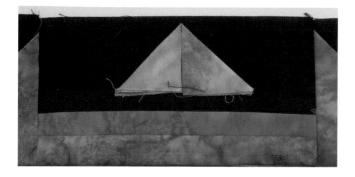 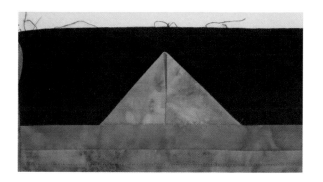

19 Fold one 9 cm (**3½″**) **Yellow** square into a triangle (Stages 10 - 11, page 14) BUT don't trim the corners off.

20 Tuck this shape under the **Orange** fold. Stitch in place by hand or machine - for stitch advice see page 8. Repeat on the other three sides.

21 Take one 5 x 7.5 cm (**2 x 3″**) **Purple** strip and fold 1.25 cm (½″) over to W/S along one long edge. Following the picture, fold to form a triangle then fold over the opposite corners of the triangle so that they overlap each other in the centre. Baste the layers along the raw edge.

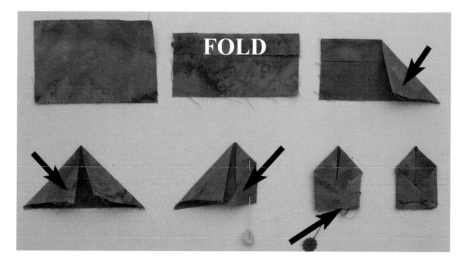

22 Tuck this shape into the pocket at the back of the **Green** triangle. Stitch in place.

23 Roll the folded edge of the centre **Green** triangle and sew in place. Roll the edge back as far as the fabric will go before the surface distorts. Repeat this on each corner of the central panel.

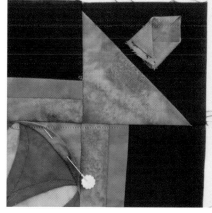 

24 Bingo - you've done it! Give yourself a gold star!

Now make another... not likely!!

Button

→

Weigh Too Much

Not only do you have to ensure there are no sharp objects nor any liquids or gels (above 100 ml in size) in your hand baggage but you have make certain that any checked bags are the right size and weight, otherwise you can be charged an extortionate fee for the excess poundage. Airline staff are remarkably good at extracting money from unwary passengers. I spend a long time weighing all my quilts and packing my checked baggage so it conforms to the regulations, although there are occasions when my carry-on may not be quite the correct weight despite being exactly the right size. Many times, I have turned down a kind offer to lift my case into the overhead bin as I knew full well that this action could precipitate a hernia. So you thank the person sweetly and announce that you much prefer to use your bag as a foot rest whilst you shove it firmly under the seat in front.

Recently, my carry-on was weighed due to some new regulation and I was rumbled. Whoops - the bag was only double the permitted amount.

"Aaah" said the young man, "You will have to pay an excess baggage charge on this."

"What if I can dispose of some of the weight?" I replied.

"Madam, you may do what you wish but the bag must only weigh 7 kgs."

Now highly suspicious of my attempt to contravene the regulations, he weighed my large light-weight case which was filled with all my quilts and lesson preparation. To his irritation it weighed exactly what was permitted - 50 lbs. He frowned and I smirked. Never ever smirk! He glared at me and reminded me that my checked luggage might be the correct weight but I had better do something about the excess poundage in my carry-on

OK - here's the answer. Find two carrier bags (buy something very small like a packet of tissues from nearest shop and insist on two bags), remove your coat and cardigan, fill both the carrier bags with the excess stuff from your carry-on, place one set of carrier bag handles over each shoulder, re-button your cardigan, zip up your coat and return to check-in. I found walking slightly difficult and really rather waddled back to the desk. I had also not appreciated that the extra padding under my arms would increase my chest size to such a wondrous extent as I had left the desk a 34A and returned a 38DD. In the interval, the over-zealous airline guy had forgotten exactly what I looked like on our first meeting, and after giving me a somewhat puzzled glance and weighing everything again - my bags and I passed scrutiny. He dispatched me to Fast Bag Drop to get the big bag of quilts tagged ready for departure.

Waddling up to the designated desk and pushing my bag onto to the luggage belt, the bag tag chap commented on the weight of my large bag.

"I am surprised", he said "That bag doesn't weigh that much it only weighs 43 lbs".

I was amazed - how could my bag have lost weight in that short time? "That's funny; the other guy said it was 50 lbs."

"Oh madam, don't worry, their scales are often wrong."

"That's good as I have one or two other things that still need to be packed."

Without more ado, I unzipped coat, unbuttoned cardigan and shoved the excess books into the bag. The bag trundled off down the belt and I left to go to the departure gate. If the Fast Bag chap had ever wondered why someone would carry books under their arms he never commented. My luggage arrived intact at my destination although now sported a large label saying "Heavy 57 lbs" but no-one asked for excess baggage fees.

On this rare occasion, I won!

Girandole

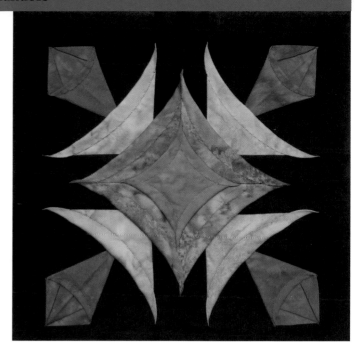

31.5 cm (12½″) including outer S/A

Cut

Four 15 cm (5⁷/₈″) squares - **Black**
Four 4 x 14 cm (1½ x 5½″) strips - **Black**
Four 4 x 16.5 cm (1½ x 6½″) strips - **Black**
Four 11.5 cm (4½″) squares - **Red**
Four 11.5 cm (4½″) squares - **Yellow**
Four 11.5 cm (4½″) squares - **Green**
One 12.5 cm (5″) square - **Orange**

Start Stitching

Seam Allowance 0.75 cm (¼″)

1 Press one **Red** square on both diagonals (R/S out). Both creases are on the R/S of the material.

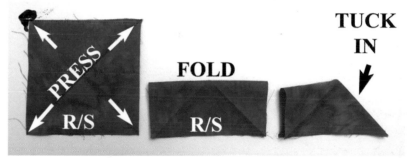

2 Fold the square into a rectangle R/S out. Working along the folded edge of the rectangle tuck one corner inwards.

The next stage seems complicated but just go slowly and look at the photographs.

3 Tuck the other corner of the folded edge inwards to form a triangle. There are now two triangular shaped folds on both sides of the shape at **A** and **B**. Lift the top triangular fold at **A** and bring it over to touch **B**. There are now three folds at **B** and only one at **A**. Not that difficult - assuming that is… you can count!

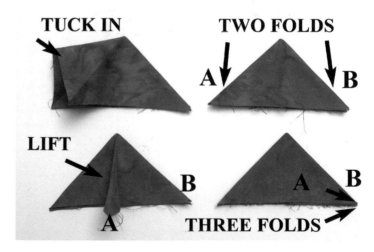

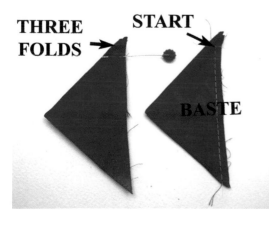

4 Arrange the three folds so that all the folded edges are flush. Pin in place. Baste along the raw edges.

Start basting at the three fold end. Lower the machine needle straight through all fabric layers before engaging the presser foot. The action of securing all the layers with the needle before lowering the presser foot will prevent the layers sliding. Keep the three folded edges exactly aligned or it might not be 'f' for fold but 'f' for fiddlesticks if the folds aren't flush!

75

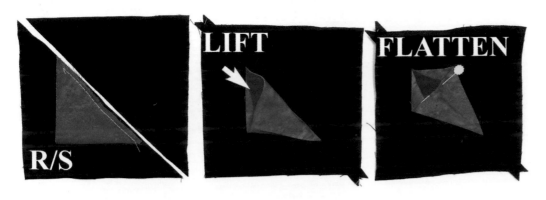

5 Cut one **Black** 15 cm (**5 ⅞″**) square in half diagonally forming two triangles.

Take one **Black** triangle R/S up and place the **Red** triangle in the centre, aligning the raw basted edge of this triangle with the diagonal side of the **Black** triangle.

To find the centre of the Black triangle, fold it in half and finger-press firmly to make a crease. The tip of the Red triangle will lie on this crease.

Pin the **Red** triangle in place. Lay the second **Black** triangle on top R/S, together. Sew the diagonal edge. Take care not to stretch this edge as you sew. Press the seam open and flat. On the R/S lift up the **Red** triangle, open out and flatten into a 'kite' shape. Tweak the layers in the centre slightly and a triangular shape will appear which covers the seam - for emphasis, this has been coloured slightly darker in the photograph above.

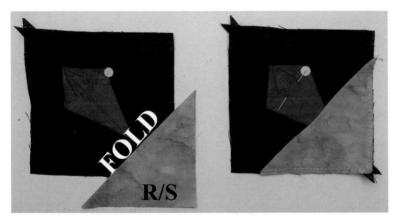

6 Press one **Yellow** 11.5 cm (**4½″**) square diagonally in half R/S out. Place on the corner of the **Black** square, pin and baste in place.

Check the yellow triangle is on the correct corner - it should be across the pointed end of the kite shape, not the blunt end!

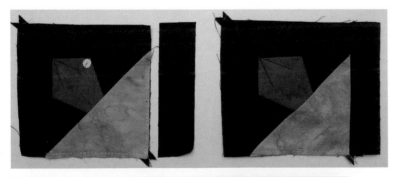

7 Attach one **Black** 4 x 14 cm (**1½ x 5½″**) strip to one side of the square. Press the seam towards the outside edge.

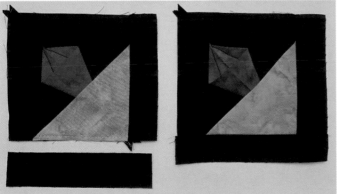

8 Attach one **Black** 4 x 16.5 cm (**1½ x 6½″**) strip to the other side as shown. Press the seam towards the outside edge.

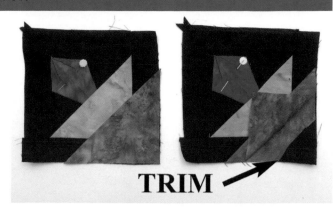

9 Press one **Green** 11.5 cm (4½") square in half diagonally R/S out, forming a triangle.

10 Before you place the **Green** triangle in place - it is advisable to trim part of the underside to reduce bulk in the final construction process.

11 Baste round the raw edge.

12 Follow Stages 1 - 9 and make three more squares. Arrange the completed sections as shown.

Now the next bit is a trifle tricky - you could join these squares together to form a larger square and omit the 12.5 cm (5") **Orange** square from the centre of the design - if so just skip the next few stages (see page 80). Alternatively, you can go for gold and complete the design by inserting the **Orange** square in the centre. For those who have made the Bow-tie patchwork this is much the same principle and you should find the technique relatively easy, if you haven't tried this patchwork - just follow the photographs closely. It will work, I promise, so continue reading and have a go!

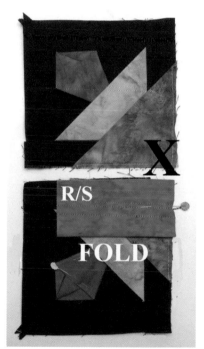

13 Fold the **Orange** 12.5 cm (5") square in half, R/S out, forming a rectangle. Place this folded rectangle on one of the completed **Black** squares as shown. The raw edges of the rectangle are aligned with the **Black** square at **X**.

14 Place another completed **Black** square on top R/S down, aligning all raw edges at **X**. Sew both sections together. Start the stitching 1.25 cm (½") away from **X**. <u>Leave a gap!</u> Sew to the end of the seam.

15 Fold back both of the **Black** squares revealing the **Orange** folded rectangle.

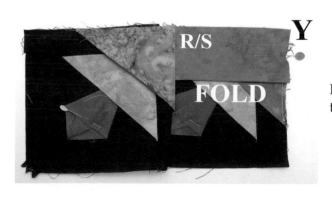

Put one of the remaining **Black** squares at the back of the folded rectangle aligning all the raw edges at **Y**.

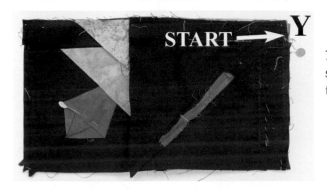

16 Place the last **Black** square on top. Commence stitching 1.25 cm (½″) away from **Y** - leave a gap! Sew to the end of the seam.

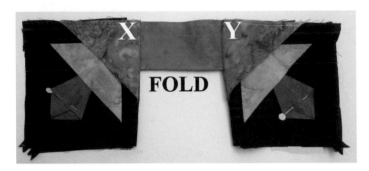

17 If you open the both sides out, they are now connected by the folded **Orange** rectangle which forms a small pocket. This is a bit like a 'bridge' between the two sections. It is a 'Bridge Over Troubled Waters' if you feel like you are struggling - panic not, at this stage you are nearly there!

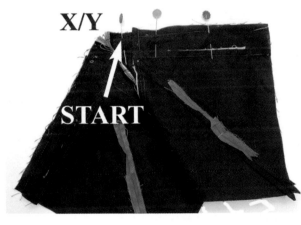

18 Open out the pocket and bring the seamed sides of the pocket at **X** and **Y** to meet. On one side of this junction align the un-sewn sides of both squares, making sure that the folded edge of the **Orange** rectangle is enclosed in the seam. Pin carefully.

19 Stitch along the seam, starting the stitching 1.25 cm (½″) from **X/Y** - leave a gap again! Sew to the end of the seam.

Almost finished!

20 Align the last two sides of the **Black** squares. Make sure that the folded edge of the **Orange** rectangle is also aligned with the sides of the **Black** squares. This might be a bit of a jiggle!

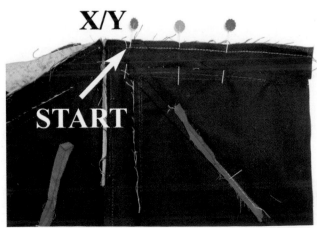

21 Sew the last seam and once more start the stitching 1.25 cm (½″) from **X/Y** - leave a gap! Sew to the end of the seam.

22 Turn over and be amazed - there is an **Orange** square magically inserted into the middle of the block (that is what should have happened - if not something has gone wrong!). Press the seams in the centre as flat as possible.

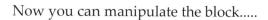

Now you can manipulate the block.....

Secure the corners of the **Red** kite shape with a few small stitches.

Roll back the edge of the **Red** shape and all the other folded edges and pin in place.

Stitch all the rolled back edges in place by hand or machine (see page 8 again).

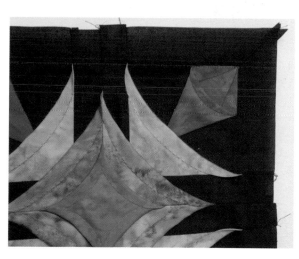

That is it - all done! Phew!

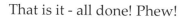

Play Time

At Stage 11, arrange the four blocks in a different way. Sew them together then roll whichever folded edges you choose.

Alternatively, go for a simpler form of the Girandole design. Forget the complicated folding in Stages 1 - 4 page 75 for the **Red** squares and fold these squares following Stages 1 - 2 page 33. Make the blocks up following Stages 5 - 12 pages 76 - 77.

1 Join the four blocks together to make a square.

2 Cut a 10 cm (**4″**) square of wadding/batting. Lay this in the centre and put the remaining 12.5 cm (**5″**) square on top.

3 Secure the kite shapes on the corners and then roll all the folded edges back and stitch in place (page 79).

The raw edges of the centre square are covered by this action.

Adding borders and a bit of decorative stitching will make an attractive cushion or quilt block.

Starburst

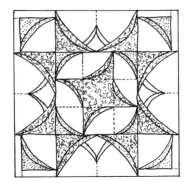

31.5 cm (**12½″**) including outer S/A's

Cut
Five 6.5 cm (**2½″**) squares - **Yellow**
Four 6.5 cm (**2½″**) squares - **Purple**
Four 7.5 cm (**3″**) squares - **Purple**
Eight 9 cm (**3½″**) squares - **Orange**
Four 6.5 x 11.5 cm (**2½ x 4½″**) strips - **Green**
Eight 6.5 cm (**2½″**) squares - **Black** + Eight 9 cm (**3½″**) squares - **Black**
Four 3 x 7.5 cm (**1 x 3″**) strips - **Black** + Four 3 x 9 cm (**1 x 3½″**) strips - **Black**

Start Stitching
Seam Allowance 0.75 cm (**¼″**)

Most of the cut squares in this design are pressed into triangles; trim part of the corner off the underside of each triangle to reduce bulk in the seams. Ensure that the triangle is placed trimmed side down or there will be a raw edge in the wrong place. You will be a most unhappy bunny if this happens!

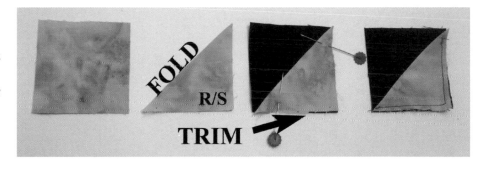

1 Press one **Yellow** 6.5 cm (**2½″**) square in half diagonally R/S out. Trim part of the back, pin and baste to one **Black** 6.5 cm (**2½″**) square. Baste the raw edges - keep the basting close to raw edge. Repeat this stage three more times making four squares in total.

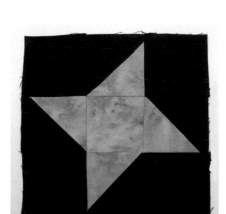

2 Take the remaining **Yellow** and four **Black** 6.5 cm (**2½″**) squares and arrange as shown.

3 Sew the nine squares together. Follow the sewing sequence as shown on page 28. Press seams open and flat. Remove any basting that is visible on the R/S of the finished block.

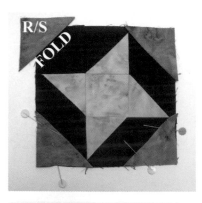

4 Press all four **Purple** 6.5 cm (2½″) squares in half diagonally forming triangles, R/S out. Trim part of the back of the triangle. (See the previous page.)

5 Place one of these triangles on each of the four corners. Pin in place and baste along the raw edges.

6 Fold one **Green** 6.5 x 11.5 cm (2½ x 4½″) strip in half R/S out. Place on R/S of one **Black** 9 cm (3½″) square as shown. Pin in place. Lay another **Black** 9 cm (3½″) square on top, R/S together and sew the seam.

7 Press the seam open and flat. Turn to R/S, lift the inserted rectangle, open it out and arrange as a triangle. Press in place and pin the corners. Make three more identical sections.

8 Press two **Orange** 9 cm (3½″) squares in half diagonally, R/S out. Trim part of the back off the triangle to reduce bulk in the seams. Place one of these trimmed triangles on either side of this section aligning all raw edges. The **Orange** triangles will overlap each other on the seam allowance.

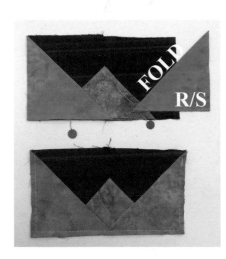

Pin and baste them in place. Repeat this three more times.

9 Press one **Purple** 7.5 cm (3″) square in half diagonally R/S out, align the raw edges, pin and baste to one **Black** 7.5 cm (3″) square.

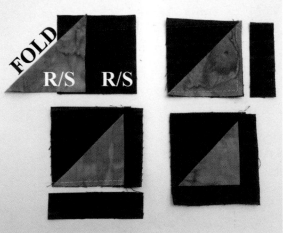

Sew one **Black** 3 x 7.5 cm (1 x 3″) strip to one side. Attach one **Black** 3 x 9 cm (1 x 3½″) strip to the other side. Remove any visible basting and press seams open and as flat as possible. Repeat three more times.

10 Arrange all the pieces as shown in the photograph.

11 Sew the sides to centre panel first then join all four sections of the top and bottom strips.

12 Sew the top and bottom strips in place. Press well. Remove any visible basting.

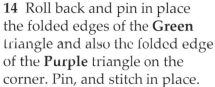

13 Roll back the folded edges of the **Purple** and **Yellow** triangles. Pin them in place and then secure using (guess what!!) the Blind Hem stitch or similar appliqué one (page 8) or... you could do it by hand - the stitching that is!

14 Roll back and pin in place the folded edges of the **Green** triangle and also the folded edge of the **Purple** triangle on the corner. Pin, and stitch in place.

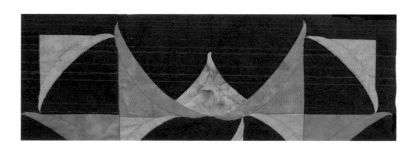

15 Lastly - Roll back, pin and stitch the folded edge of all the **Orange** triangles.

Play Time

Tuck small folded rectangles (Stage 21, page 73) under the **Purple** or **Yellow** triangles.

For a subtly different textured effect try stuffing a little padding into the pocket underneath each of the triangles.

Add beads and buttons for extra embellishment.

At Stage 10 rearrange the pieces in a different pattern before sewing together and rolling back all the folded edges.

Stars for Us!

97 cm (**38"**) square

The main panel of this small quilt is made from nine 22.5 cm (**9"**) blocks. The block design comes from the centre section of Starburst (pages 81 - 82). Three colours were chosen and two different arrangements of these colours were used to create the completed pattern.

Materials
85 x 115 cm (**33 x 44"**) strip - **Blue**
75 x 115 cm (**30 x 44"**) strip - **Red**
75 x 115 cm (**30 x 44"**) strip - **Cream**
105 cm (**42"**) square backing fabric
105 cm (**42"**) square wadding/batting
7.5 cm (**3"**) square stiff paper/thin card

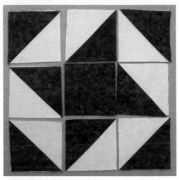

Cut
Seventy two 9 cm (**3½"**) squares - **Cream**
Forty one 9 cm (**3½"**) squares - **Red**
Forty 9 cm (**3½"**) squares - **Blue**

1 Follow Stages 1 - 5, pages 81 - 82 and make nine blocks. Arrange the colours of the squares as shown in the photographs. Make **four** blocks with a **Blue** centre and **five** blocks with a **Red** centre.

2 Arrange all nine blocks as a large square and sew together.

3 Measure the sides of the quilt and cut four 4.5 cm (**1¾"**) **Red** strips and four 13 cm (**5¼"**) **Blue** strips the same length. Join one **Red** and one **Blue** strip together to form a wide band. Repeat with the remaining strips, and make three more bands.

4 Stitch one of these bands to opposite sides of the quilt.

5 Cut four **Red** 16 cm (**6½"**) squares. Stitch one **Red** square to either end of the remaining two bands. Sew one band to the top and one band to the bottom of the quilt. Press well.

6 Roll back all the folded edges of the **Red** and **Blue** triangles and sew in place.

7 Fold the 7.5 cm (3″) of stiff paper/thin card in half diagonally; draw an arc shape; cut the drawn line; open out and amazingly there is a heart shape.

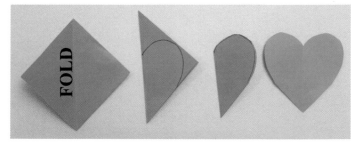

8 Pin the paper heart to the back of the **White** fabric. Cut approximately 1 cm ($^3/_8$″) outside the heart shape. Clip the curves very carefully especially at the 'cleavage' of the heart. Fold the excess fabric over the edge of the paper and press. Baste the fabric to the paper.

To get a good crisp outline of the heart shape, use spray starch and a small paintbrush. Spray the starch solution into a small saucer/tin lid or dish. Dip the brush in the liquid and moisten the edge of the fabric before pressing over the paper.
(Tip from Dawn Cameron-Dick)

9 Stitch the heart to the **Red** corner square by hand or select one of the machine appliqué stitches (page 8). Repeat on the other three corners.

Remove the basting from the heart shape before turning to the W/S of the panel. Cut a slit in the back of the heart. The paper should fall out - if not a good tug helps!

10 For a pleasing tactile finish, pad the heart shape.

Insert some small pieces of polyester stuffing or torn fragments of wadding. Poke the padding through the hole in the back, spreading the stuffing evenly. A small barbecue skewer or stiletto makes a good poker. Stitch the hole up roughly to retain the padding.

11 Lay the panel on the wadding and backing square. Pin/baste or Tak-gun the three layers together before commencing any quilting. Sew round the outer edge of the quilted panel before trimming any excess backing and wadding. Bind the raw edge.

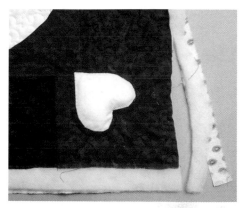

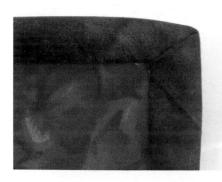

Mitred Binding

There are several ways to bind a quilt and you may have your own special method. Here is an easy way to make a 1.25 cm (½") binding with mitred corners on the front and on the back of the quilt.

To make the binding, cut four 5 x 115 cm (**2 x 44"**) strips - cut these strips across the fabric from selvedge to selvedge. Join all the strips with a narrow seam to form one long length. Press the seams open and flat. Do not fold the strip in half - leave it flat.

Start in the centre of one side: On the R/S of the quilt, align the raw edge of the binding exactly with the edge of the quilt (R/S of binding to R/S of quilt). Leave approximately 7 cm (3") of the binding strip unattached (as shown on page 17) before starting to stitch. Sew the binding in place with 1.25 cm (½") seam allowance.

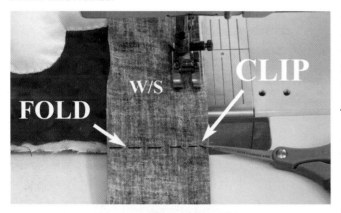

Setting 1.25 cm (½") S/A on your sewing machine: Align the fabric edge with 1.25 cm (½") line marked on the throat plate. Alternatively, move the needle to the extreme left of the presser foot and if necessary set the presser foot in by a tiny amount from the edge of the fabric so that the distance between the needle and the edge of the material equals 1.25 cm (½"). If neither method works, measure 1.25 cm (½") from the needle position, stick a small piece of masking tape on the throat plate at this distance and use this as a guide for the fabric edge.

Stop sewing approximately 5 - 7 cm (**2 - 3"**) from the corner of the quilt, and lower the needle into the fabric to prevent the layers moving. Make a small clip in the edge of the binding fabric level with the edge of the quilt. Fold and crease the binding fabric R/S together on the tiny clip. Turn the folded binding at a right angle so that the raw edge of the binding strips aligns with the next side of the quilt - a small triangle is formed in the binding strip.

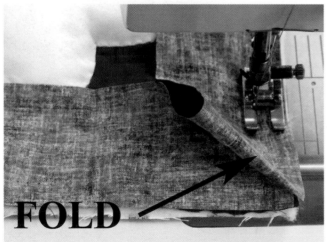

Turn this triangle from one side to the other to create a firm and clearly marked crease across the base as shown in the photograph.

Continue stitching and sew up to the crease. Stop stitching exactly on the crease.

DO NOT GO ONE STITCH FURTHER.
It will be a stitch too far!

Raise the needle and fold the triangle over to the other side. Re-commence the sewing on the crease line - use 1.25 cm (½″) S/A. Ideally both lines of stitch will meet at right-angles - each line either side of the crease at the base of the triangle.

Keep going until all corners have been completed.

Once the binding has been attached to the quilt the ends of the binding need to be joined. This can be done by hand, or try the following technique:

1 At the start of the binding a small portion of the strip was left unstitched; repeat this manoeuvre at the end and leave a small portion of the binding unstitched.

2 Fold back the start and the finish of the loose binding ends so that the both folds are flush with each other. Crease the folds well and align the two creases.

3 Join the pieces by stitching them together on the creased fold line. With a bit of a wriggle and a jiggle these ends can be joined by machine unless you prefer to sew them together by hand.

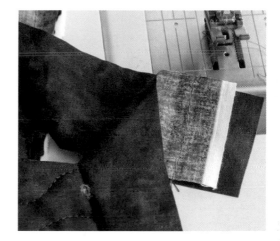

4 Trim the excess fabric to 0.75 cm (¼″) from the seam. Re-align the edge of the binding with the edge of the quilt. Complete the stitching.

To form the mitred corner on the R/S of the quilt, fold the binding to the back of the work. Fold the binding fabric at 1.25 cm (½″) from the stitching. Once the binding is folded over to the back of the quilt, incredibly, a mitred corner will appear on the front of the quilt.

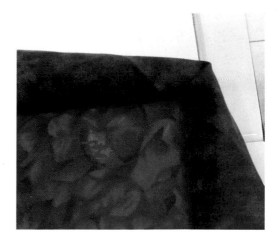

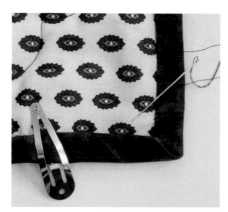

Turn the quilt over, and with a careful bit of tweaking and jiggling a mitred corner can be created on the back as well. Turn the raw edge under and slip stitch in place.

P.S. Quilt clips or hair grips are very good for holding the binding in place while you sew along the folded edge.

There you are - mitred binding - easy-peasy, lemon squeezy!

Travel Tips from a Traumatised Twiddler

Check your ticket

Read the words and check where you are going before you complete any purchase of your flights. Some airport names can be confusing. Beware, one or two of the cheapest airlines fly to some airports situated miles from your destination then it costs a fortune to get a taxi to your hotel.

Some time ago, I was teaching in Rochester, Minnesota, scheduled to fly back to Heathrow. I had checked my ticket or so I thought. I was dropped off at the airport in plenty of time for my flight then discovered to my absolute horror that my ticket was from Rochester but the letters 'NY' beside the city name did not refer to name of airport but to name of state. I had a ticket from Rochester New York not Rochester Minnesota - only 1000 miles away! Panic struck as I had promised my mother to be back in time for her 'bionic' knee operation the next day.

The only solution: Buy another ticket and fly twenty four hours later, going via Rochester to Minneapolis to Chicago to Detroit to Amsterdam and then back to Heathrow at an extra cost of $1285.15. Oh Joy! There is nothing more miff making than to fly over one's mother undergoing the chop in deepest Wales then over my own home to Amsterdam then return to Heathrow. But Schiphol Airport is a most splendid airport serving the best cup of coffee I had had in a long time. There is always a bright side if you can look hard enough.

Read the regulations

Clearing Immigration in another country can prove a minefield to the unwary. You must obey any entry requirements as defined on the landing card and remember that many foodstuffs are not permitted in any form in most countries.

Houston airport was the scene of my first arrest. I had ignored the rule about NO FRUIT permitted in the USA and had kept a couple of apples in my carry-on (as I might not be able to buy fresh fruit in downtown Houston). It took ages to get through Immigration and by the time I got to the baggage carousel my bags were sitting on the concourse. Two armed guards were standing with their sniffer dogs beside the luggage. "Mam, you have meat in these bags?", they enquired. Meat? I'm a veggie so this wasn't possible but it suddenly dawned that I had cushion covers in the cases and they had had feather pads inside. The dogs could smell the feathers - hence they thought there might be chickens or ducks inside my cases. As I explained the situation to the two stern-faced belligerent looking guys, the dogs turned their attention to me and sniffed at my carry-on. They could smell the apples.

Ah-ha - the armed guards pounced - I was guilty - they were right. At gun-point, I was marched through to another department where all my bags were searched and put through a special machine. As my carry-on emerged (minus the two apples), it fell landing heavily on the concrete floor. My duty-free bottle of brandy inside the case broke. All my clothes and other personal items were covered in broken glass and saturated with alcohol.

A little while later, I checked into my somewhat up-market hotel, still leaking brandy and smelling like a distillery. The reception staff raised polite eyebrows but said nothing despite the trail of liquid following my passage across the lobby. On reaching my bedroom and unpacking the case, hidden in the corner was a third apple somewhat brandy soaked! Completely overlooked by all the special x-ray machines and security guards. I ate it very hastily.

Rambling Roses:
Ngaire Lang
Specially made for Rosie in New Zealand. by Ngaire, her New Zealand aunt.

Whirlygig

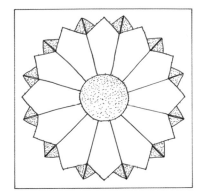

31.5 cm (**12½″**) including outer S/A

Cut

One 31.5 cm (**12½″**) square - **Black**
One 11 x 46 cm (**4½ x 18″**) strip - **Purple**
Twelve 4.5 cm (**3″**) squares - **Green**
One 10 cm (**4″**) square - **Green**
One 11 x 46 cm (**4½ x 18″**) strip - **Orange**

Whirlygig Template

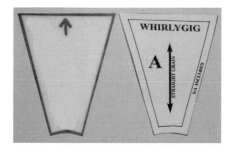

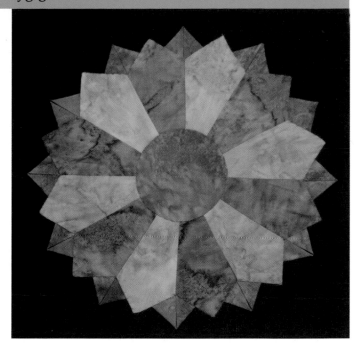

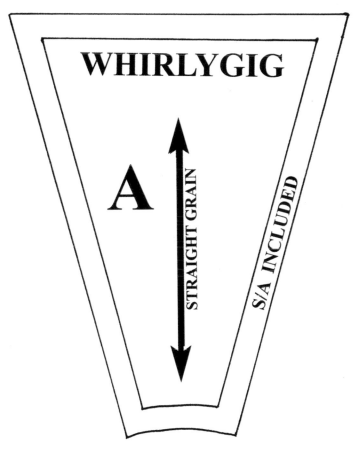

Trace the outline of Template **A** on to some form of thin or opaque paper such as baking parchment, greaseproof or tracing paper. Cut the shape out roughly then glue the paper to thin card. Alternatively, trace the template on template plastic or any transparent material that can be cut with scissors or the rotary cutter. Cut the shape out exactly on the outside line. (Beware, if you choose to photocopy as opposed to tracing the template, sometimes the photocopy is inaccurate.)

Place the template on to the W/S of the fabric aligning the straight grain line on the template with the straight grain of the fabric. Draw round the template using a hard sharp pencil. Slant the pencil at 45° to the template edge to get the tip of the pencil really close to the side. Remove the template and carefully cut the fabric. Cut on the inner side of drawn line as the drawn line is actually outside the template.

Alternatively, cut round the template with the rotary cutter, be careful not to slice small portions off the card or your fingers. Adding a thick black line to the edge of the template is advisable. If the black line gets thinner, you have cut bits off the template and/or your fingers.

A small piece of double sided sticky tape is very useful for securing the template to the fabric and prevents it shifting on the slippery surface of the fabric when you cut. Keep the piece of non-stick paper (from the tape), and re-cover the sticky side of tape afterward so the template is prepared for the next time you wish to use it. (Clover MFG. Co. Ltd. make a double sided basting tape which could be used instead.)

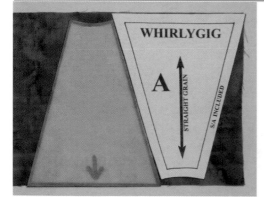

Start Stitching
Seam Allowance 0.65 cm (¼″)
(**N.B. Metric S/A is 0.65 cm not 0.75 cm for this pattern**)

1 Cut six Template **A** in **Purple** and six in **Yellow** from the 11 x 46 cm (4½ x 18″) strips. Alternate the direction of the template to save fabric and cutting time.

2 Fold one **Purple** shape in half W/S together. Press the fold lightly. Sew across the end as shown using 0.65 cm (¼″) S/A. Clip the corner off the seam.

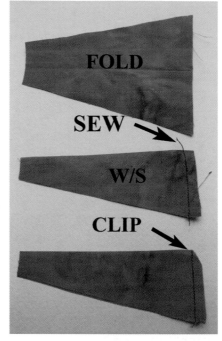

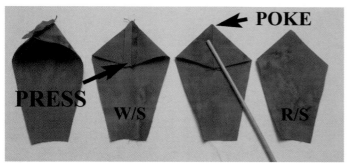

3 Press the seam open. Turn the stitched section R/S out.

Poke the end out gently to form a soft point. The blunt end of a barbecue skewer is ideal for this operation. Align the seam with the first lightly pressed crease. Press again.

4 Make eleven more using the remaining **Purple** and **Yellow** pieces.

5 Sew one **Purple** section to one **Yellow** section. Repeat five more times. Sew from the outer edge toward the centre.

Secure the thread ends by using the lock stitch button on your machine at the start of the seam (see your instruction book) or begin the stitching approximately 1 cm (½″) into the seam, reverse to the start of the seam and sew to the end.

Sew the two sections together in the same order i.e. **Purple** underneath and **Yellow** on top or vice versa. Consistency pays!

Remember to sew an accurate 0.65 cm (¼″) S/A. Don't press the seams yet!

6 Sew the sets of two sections into sets of four sections. Make three.

7 Sew these three sections together to form a circle.

8 Lay the circle onto the R/S of the **Black** 31.5 cm (**12½″**) square.

To centre the design, press the Black square in eighths - in half from corner to corner (diagonally) and from side to side. Alternatively rule light lines in the same pattern, using a chalk or removable marker.

Position the circle so the pressed or drawn lines bisect the seams and the points of the design.

B

WHIRLYGIG

ADD SEAM ALLOWANCE TO FABRIC

This is an excellent way to get any applied design exactly in the middle of a square without a lot of measuring.

9 Trace round Template **B** and cut out in stiff paper or card. Check that the template covers all the raw edges of the centre of the Whirlygig block - if not - cut another circle a little larger.

10 Pin the template to the back of the **Green** 10 cm (**4″**) square. Cut the fabric approximately 1 cm (½″) away from the template edge. Clip the outer edge of the fabric carefully before pressing it over the edge of the template. (See spray starch tip on page 85.) Baste the fabric to the paper using the longest stitch length on your machine.

A small wooden stick such as a bamboo barbecue skewer or the point of the stitch ripper or small scissors is useful for feeding/pushing the folds under the presser foot as you sew round.

11 Pin the fabric covered template to the centre of the design.

12 Sew the centre in place either by hand or machine using some form of appliqué stitch (see page 8 for suggestions).

13 Remove the basting from the centre. Turn over and trim the **Black** fabric 0.65 cm (¼″) away from the stitching. The paper will fall out, if not - a gentle tug might be necessary.

14 Fold a 6.5 cm (2½″) **Green** square into a smaller square as shown. Sew a few stitches in the corner to hold the folds together. Make eleven more.

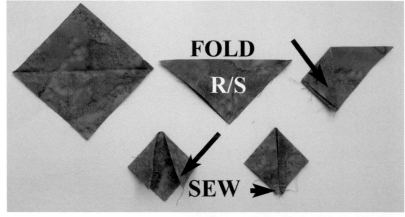

15 Tuck these shapes under the outside edge of the Whirlygig design. Stitch the shapes in place. If you haven't guessed already, see page 8 for stitch suggestions!

Play Time

Sew the tip of the inserted **Green** square to the **Black** fabric then roll back the two sides of the centre fold. Stitch in place. Alternatively, omit the **Green** inserts and tuck lace, braid or a frill under the outside edge of the design instead.

Stuff the centre of the block by laying a small circle of wadding/batting underneath before pinning the Whirlygig to the **Black** square. Why not embellish the centre with beads and embroidery or add some lace around the centre circle?

Experiment with fabric printed in wide/narrow stripes. Cut the **A** template both vertically and horizontally on some striped material. The resulting arrangements of the stripes might make one's eyes go squiffy, or was that the wine!

Basic Bag

Approx. 48 cm (**19"**) square

Sew two seams and create a bag with a base - a flat bottom! What could be easier? This follows a very simple principle which enables the bag proportions to be adjusted easily to specific needs. (See Stage 3 below.) You can choose to have a bigger bottom or a smaller bottom… to the bag of course! From six to sixty-six years old and more - this handy carrier can be made by anyone for all.

For preference, select a crisp fabric with some 'body' such as glazed cotton, heavy calico (muslin in US) or good quality batik.

Materials

One Whirlygig design (optional)
One 50 x 115 cm (**20 x 44"**) strip - bag
Two 7.5 x 50 cm (**3 x 20"**) strips - handles
Thread to match fabric

1 Make up one Whirlygig design to Stages 1 - 7 pages 90 - 91. Attach the centre following Stages 9 - 12 pages 91 - 92. Remove the basting from the centre section and pull the paper out from the back.

2 Fold the 50 x 115 cm (**20 x 44"**) strip in half, R/S out. Press the folded edge.

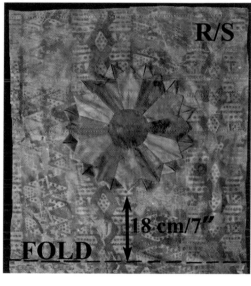

Open out again. Pin the Whirlygig design on the R/S of the single layer bag strip, setting it approximately 18 cm (**7"**) from the <u>folded</u> edge. Tuck the folded inserts underneath the outside edge of the Whirlygig before appliquéing the design to the material.

3 Re-fold the bag fabric W/S out. Tuck the pressed folded edge 6 cm (**2½"**) inwards. Check the depth of the folded tuck measures the same at both ends.

At this point you can choose the size of the bag bottom/base. For a bigger bottom - tuck in more than 6 cm (**2½"**), for a smaller bottom reduce the size of this tuck. Oh that life could be so simple!

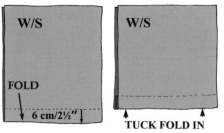

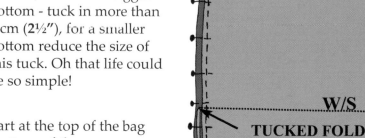

4 Pin the tucked fold and the sides. Start at the top of the bag and sew over the folded layers to the bottom of the seam.

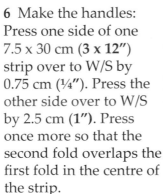

5 Overlocking (serging) the raw edge of the side seams will prevent fraying.

6 Make the handles: Press one side of one 7.5 x 30 cm (**3 x 12"**) strip over to W/S by 0.75 cm (**¼"**). Press the other side over to W/S by 2.5 cm (**1"**). Press once more so that the second fold overlaps the first fold in the centre of the strip.

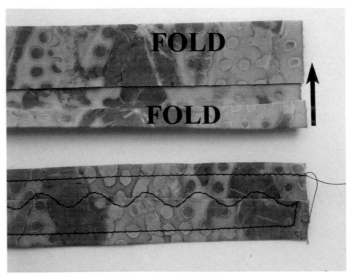

7 Sew along the centre fold using some form of decorative pattern, then stitch down the sides.

8 Repeat with the other strip to make the second handle.

9 On the top of the bag, fold the raw edge over 1.25 cm (**½"**) to W/S. Tuck the ends of one handle underneath this folded edge. Space the handle ends at one-third intervals, measuring along the top of one side of the bag. Pin in place. Position the other handle on the other side of the bag at the same intervals and pin in place.

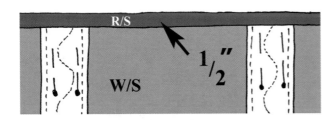

10 Fold the top of the bag approximately 5 cm (**1"**) over the handle ends. Pin in place. Sew round the top of the bag. In addition, top stitch round the edge for extra strength.

11 Turn the bag R/S out. Put your hand into the corner of the bag bottom and push the fold outwards to form a triangular fold. Repeat on the other corner. These two triangular shapes magically create a flat base to the bag.

12 Take the bag and go shopping - nothing like a little retail therapy!

This simple principle can be adopted for any sized strip of material. The depth of the tucked fold will define the width of the base of the bag. For a bigger bottomed bag - tuck a larger amount in and vice versa for a bag with a narrow base. The handle length can be altered to suit, or you could contemplate making one long handle and attaching one end to each side seam.

Twirling Pinwheel

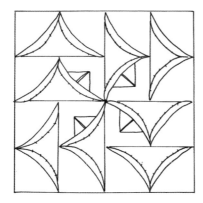

31.5 cm (**12½″**) including outer S/A

Cut
Sixteen 9 cm (**3½″**) squares - **Black**
Four 9 x 16.5 cm (**3½ x 6½″**) strips - **Orange**
Four 9 x 16.5 cm (**3½ x 6½″**) strips - **Green**
Four 7.5 cm (**3″**) squares - **Yellow**

Start Stitching
Seam Allowance 0.75 cm (**¼″**)

1 Take one 9 cm (**3½″**) x 16.5 cm (**6½″**) **Orange** strip and fold in half, R/S out. Place this rectangle on to the R/S of one **Black** 9 cm (**3½″**) square, positioning the folded shape 0.75 cm (**¼″**) from the top of the square.

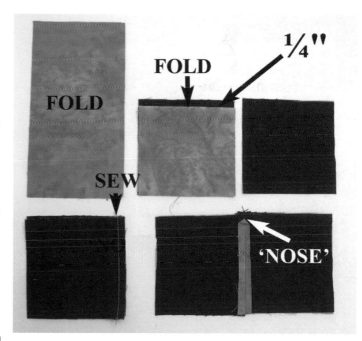

Lay another **Black** 9 cm (**3½″**) square on top. Sew one side as shown. Press the seam open and flat. Press the 'nose' (top of the **Orange** rectangle) downwards.

2 Open the **Orange** rectangle and arrange it as a triangle. The corners of the rectangle should bisect the corners of the underlying square. Pin in place before basting the raw edge.

Stages 1 - 2 are the same method as described in Skyrocket Stages 5 - 8, page 62.

3 Make three more sections using the **Orange** 9 x 16.5 cm (**3½ x 6½″**) strips and **Black** squares.

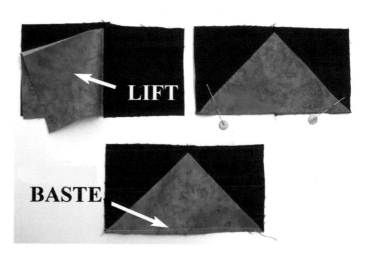

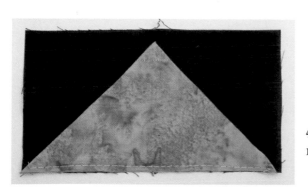

4 Make four sections using the **Green** strips and remaining **Black** squares.

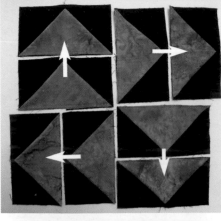

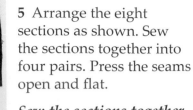

5 Arrange the eight sections as shown. Sew the sections together into four pairs. Press the seams open and flat.

Sew the sections together with the Orange triangle on the top. For an accurate point to the Orange triangle on the R/S, sew exactly past the tip of the 'nose' showing in the seam.

NOSE

6 Sew the pairs together to form both halves of the finished block.

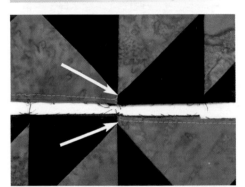

7 Match the points at the centre when sewing the two halves together. Should the points fail to meet in the centre of the completed design... Guess what? Buttons are brill!!

Ha! I achieved this perfection first go!!!

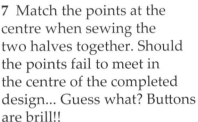

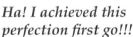

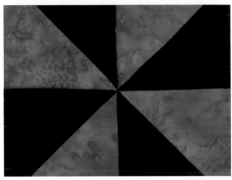

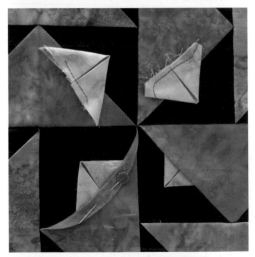

8 Fold the **Yellow** 7.5 cm (**3"**) squares into triangles (see Stages 10 - 11, page 14). Trim the corners before tucking the shapes into the pockets at the back of the **Orange** triangles. Tuck these shapes deeply into the pockets so that they will be held place when the edges of the triangles are rolled back and sewn in place.

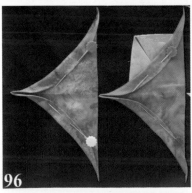

Roll back the edge of the **Orange** triangles and sew in place.

9 In addition, roll the folded edges of the **Green** triangles and stitch in place - dare I say it - see page 8 for details!

Play Time

Why not arrange the eight sections in a different pattern as displayed in the diagram?

What about changing the colour of the 9 cm (3½″) squares? Do they all have to be the same? No. Experiment with different colour arrangements and see what happens to the overall design.

How about changing the size of the sections, turning them sideways and using as a border to the main block? Flying Geese I hear you say - and indeed the effect is the same as that design but the folded edges of this technique can be rolled creating a curved outline. Much more effective!

(Flying Geese is a traditional patchwork design usually made from two sorts of triangles - half and quarter square ones. Unless you are a patchwork aficionado that will make no sense whatsoever - I would advise skipping this bit of information!)

The border of the small quilt pictured here was made from 6.5 cm (2½″) squares and 6.5 x 11.5 cm (2½ x 4½″) strips formed into sections, following Stages 1 - 2, page 95.

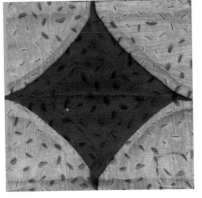

Do all these sections have to go the same way? No. Play with the pieces and turn them round. Turn two so that the shapes will join together to form a square.

Why not turn two sections so they form a square, lay a small square of contrasting coloured fabric on top, then roll the folded sides of the two sections over the raw edge of the contrasting fabric and sew in place? This is reminiscent of the central section of Cathedral Window patchwork.

Horrors of the Hotel Room

Travel Lodges and Premier Inns are pleasant to stay in as they have a similar standard of reasonably equipped good quality rooms and the bed is nearly always comfortable. Other hotel bedrooms can vary from the replica of a tart's boudoir in both appearance and smell to those so unbearably grubby that sleeping on your quilts is the only way to avoid the bedbugs which, to be honest, probably only exist in my imagination. In many hotels the staff don't do dusting - it seems to be a forgotten art, and the grim appearance of bathroom extractor fans has to be seen to be believed. Gawd, I do hate dangling grey matted cobwebs and that awful smell of a room deodourised with those dire scented plug-ins (they are a fire hazard, so remove it if you find one).

I have even been allocated a room with no bed - the hotel staff had forgotten that it had been removed for some reason, hopefully not due to an infestation of bedbugs! Another hotel had a live carpet crawling with jumpers - and these were not of the sweater variety. Quite interesting really, sitting on one's bed fully dressed with elastic bands round your trouser legs and cuffs to prevent any inadvertent ingress of the little hoppers.

Aah, but... pornography! I had never dreamt that I would spend a useful evening looking for pornographic material in my hotel room. Why, might you ask? A fellow stitcher and I were discussing hotels and the problems with finding a nice one. To my surprise, she related how her husband used to look for evidence of pornography in his room as he had inadvertently found some uncensored magazines and related oddments on one occasion behind the bed. Since that time he had searched his room thoroughly and had found more - behind the wardrobe, under the mattress, behind and inside the chest of drawers and concealed above the panels of a suspended ceiling. He had even managed to get his accommodation free due to the amount of stuff he had discovered. Wow - a free night's stay!

If you are puzzled as to why this type of material might be found hidden in a hotel room - think on. It is not a good idea to take the stuff home - your other half might not appreciate it; you can't throw it in the bin outside the hotel due to the constant CCTV surveillance outside most hotel car parks and if you left it visible in the room - how would the room maid feel?

So that night, I searched and searched. There was no wardrobe nor a suspended ceiling nor could I lift the mattress, but I could search the chest of drawers. Removing the fourth and last drawer, I struck pay dirt - literature in several forms. One piece of folded paper was the drawer fitting instructions - boring.

The other two were hefty brochures. Leaning in to the empty cabinet, I lifted the first thick magazine and read the title... "How to fit a Double Broiler". It proved to be a weighty tome on kitchen fittings for Burger King. The second slimmer brochure beckoned. Perhaps this would be my ticket for a free night's stay? No such luck. This was a promotional manual extolling the delights of selling Burger King Woppa's to the general public. You have no idea of how exciting this can be!

There was no pornographic bumf of any description, but I was so glad that I had found the drawer fitting instructions as I would never have got all four drawers back correctly without them!

Unfinished Symphony: Shelagh Jarvis
If only all hotel rooms had such nice bedding - it would be a pleasure to stay there.

Quilt Finale

Sewing the blocks together is the best bit, whether you choose to make a double bed sized quilt, a single one, a wall-hanging or a lap quilt.

On completing all the designs arrange the squares in an attractive pattern. Attempt to balance the colours and shapes to form a pleasing formation. Avoid having any similarly patterned or coloured blocks side by side or in a row.

The twelve designs in this book can be sewn together to form a 91 x 121 cm (36½ x 48½″) panel, but if a larger panel is required, why not repeat some of your favourite blocks, or select other interesting 31 cm (12½″) squares featuring other patchwork techniques and combine them all together? You are the artiste, you choose.

Once you have completed the arrangement, number the individual blocks or sketch/photograph the layout before you move the pieces. Marvellous though our memories are, you may not recall the exact layout as you start to sew the squares together: sometimes one suffers from a CRAFT moment - **C**an't **R**emember **A** **F**lipping **T**hing (this is the polite version!).

Before you go any further - make sure that all the blocks are the same-sized squares.

Trim any excess material or add a small border where necessary to achieve equal-sized squares.

Having sewn all the blocks together to form a large panel, a border or borders may be necessary to increase the overall size. To enlarge the dimensions, cut strips of fabric the desired size and attach them to the raw edges of the quilt. In my opinion it is preferable to cut these strips from selvedge to selvedge (side to side across the material) and if necessary join the strips together to make the correct measurement. Join the strips using a smaller stitch length than normal, a narrow seam allowance, and press the seam open and flat. These actions will render the seam between the cut strips less obvious.

Measure the sides of the quilt before attaching any border and cut the strips to this length and the desired width. If necessary take the average measurement of the length of the sides and cut the length to this measurement. Pin the border in place and 'ease' where needed to make the border fit each side of the quilt. Ease is a professional term for persuading the raw edges and seams to match precisely, but gremlins abound and sometimes the only way to make everything fit is a very good tug of one of the layers.

Cutting a border the correct length and making the raw quilt edge and the length of the border match up will ensure that the final measurement of the relevant sides stay even. Just cutting an indeterminate strip for a border of any length and attaching it to one side of your work without any semblance of measuring may result in distorted and unevenly measured edges.

This is an easy method of enlarging any quilt or panel but a little boring - why not increase the size of the quilt and add cohesion to the various patterns by adding strips between the blocks, or sashing as it is often called?

*Kaleidoscopes Two: 150 x 190 cm (**60 x 75"**) Jennie Rayment: Features all twelve block designs from this book with bias sashing and corner squares. Machine pieced. Machine quilted on polyester wadding.*

Sashing & Corner Squares

What is sashing? This is a framework of strips that is often used to connect blocks together in a quilt or wall-hanging. Sashing can vary from a plain strip of fabric to a complex pattern. Ideally the sashing will complement and define the block designs in addition to expanding the creative pzzazz of the overall appearance. Frequently the sashed frame work is a combination of strips of equal width but the length is cut to fit the exact dimensions of the blocks. Corner squares are required to complete the framework (see the picture on page 103).

Here is an innovative and intriguing sashing composed of bias strips laid on to a contrasting straight cut backing material. A bias strip is created by cutting the fabric at a 45° angle to a straight edge. Fabric cut on the bias can be rolled back in a curve, thus producing an interesting arced effect. (Straight cut material will not behave in the same fashion.)

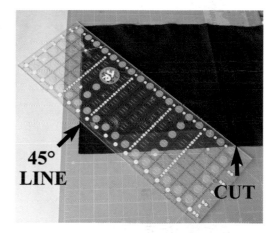

45° LINE / CUT

Cut

One 29 x 115 cm (**11½ x 45"**) strip - **Black***
One 5 x 31 cm (**2 x 12½"**) strip - **Red**
*Sufficient fabric for four 31 x 9 cm (**12½ x 3½"**) sashing bands

Preparing Bias Strips

A 50 cm (**18"**) or longer long ruler is useful when cutting these bias strips.

1 Lay the 29 x 115 cm (**11½ x 45"**) **Black** strip on a cutting mat. Align the 45° line printed on the cutting ruler along one straight side of the material. To prevent wasting the material, place the long edge of the ruler through the corner of the 29 x 115 cm (**11½ x 45"**) **Black** strip. Cut along the edge of the ruler.

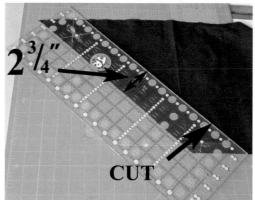

2¾" / CUT

REMOVE

This cut is now on the bias, i.e. at 45° to the straight edge.

2 Discard the small triangular section. Working on the larger portion of the fabric, measure 7 cm (**2¾"**) from the bias edge and cut a strip.

3 Using the same measurement, re-align the ruler with the bias edge and cut another strip.

4 Repeat Stage 3 until you have cut eight 7 cm (**2¾"**) wide bias cut strips.

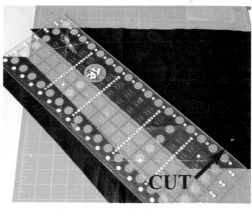

CUT

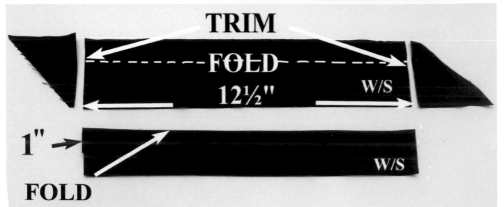

Sashing Strip

1 Trim two **Black** bias strips into 31 cm (**12½"**) lengths.

2 Fold one long side of each **Black** bias strip 2.5 cm (**1"**) over to the W/S. Press gently.

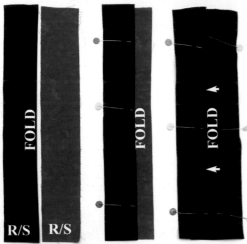

3 Fold the 5 x 31 cm (**2 x 12½"**) **Red** strip in half lengthways, and press lightly to make a crease down the centre. Open out the strip after creasing.

4 Lay one **Black** bias strip on to the **Red** 31.5 cm (**12½"**) strip butting the folded edge of bias strip to the centre crease, and pin in place.

Repeat with a second folded bias strip, ensuring that the fold of each bias strip butts up to the centre crease of the **Red** 31.5 cm (**12½"**) strip. Pin well.

5 Sew a 1.25 cm (**½"**) seam either side of the two centre folds.

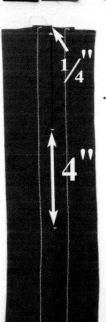

6 Measure 0.75 cm (**¼"**) along the centre folds working from each end of the strip, and mark this measurement lightly with a pencil. At this mark sew across the folds; use a small stitch length and sew back and forth across the folds to hold both edges firmly together. Mark out the remaining space at 10 cm (**4"**) intervals; secure the folds at these points with the same short stitch length.

7 On either side of the centre, roll back both folds to reveal the contrasting colour underneath. The folds roll outwards forming arcs with an oval space between. Pin the edges of the folds in place.

8 Secure the rolled edge with a few small hand or machine stitches (see page 8). Sewing round the arced edge with a contrasting coloured thread to the fabric will emphasise any deviations in the stitching line - the wobbles will show.

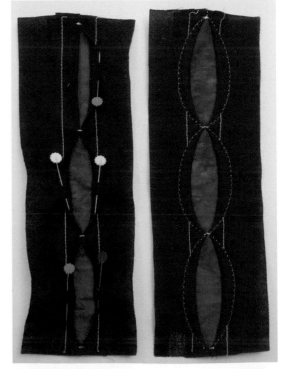

Disguise these wobbles by selecting a thread colour that tones with the material - your little deviations will be rendered almost invisible. Why not consider enhancing the arced shape by sewing the edge in place with a decorative stitch? A bit of extra embellishment can look most attractive.

That is one sashing strip made - now all you have to do is make a few more!

Save time by cutting the sashing strips in bulk. Lay several strips of fabric together in a neat pile and cut simultaneously. Press down steadily on the cutting ruler then push the rotary cutter firmly up the side of the ruler. A really sharp cutter should cut through twelve layers of fabric easily if you give it a bit of welly and a firm push!

Contemplate changing the distance between the small bar tacks/stitches across the central folds. For preference keep this distance at least 6 cm (2½″) to prevent the oval shape losing definition.

Why not consider a different colour in the centre of the sashing - do all the strips have to have the same colour in the centre?

Corner Square

These are required to complete the sashed framework. Sometimes referred to as cornerstones, the construction of this square can be a simple or complex design. There is no reason why the corner square cannot be a plain piece of material as shown in the bottom left hand corner of the photograph above - if so just cut squares the same dimension as the width of the sashing band.

As the blocks in this book feature rolled and folded fabric, here is a textured design that could be manipulated to complement the bias strip sashing. The edges of the central section of this corner square construction can be rolled back creating a similarly shaped arc to the one in the bias strip sashing.

This corner stone design consists of a **Yellow** square inserted between the seams of four **Black** squares. Confused? Don't be - just follow the pictures step by step. (This technique is the same construction method described on Girandole, pages 77 - 78.)

Cut - for one Corner Square
One 9 cm (3½″) square - **Yellow**
Four 5.25 cm (2″) squares - **Black**

Start Stitching
Seam Allowance 0.75 cm (¼″)

1 Fold the **Yellow** 9 cm (3½″) square in half forming a rectangle R/S out. Sandwich one end of this rectangle between two 5.25 cm (2″) **Black** squares, R/S of **Black** squares to R/S of **Yellow** rectangle.

Sew the layers together down the side indicated in the photograph **BUT** begin stitching 1 cm (³/₈″) from the top of the seam. **LEAVE A GAP**! Sew to the end of the material.

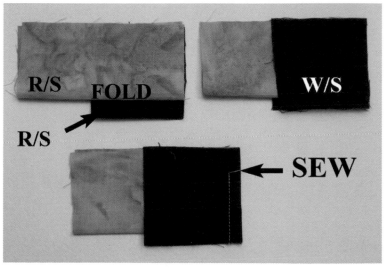

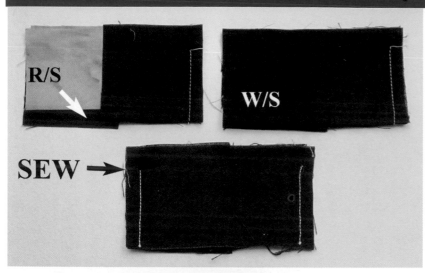

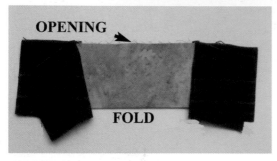

2 Place the remaining two **Black** squares on the other end of the rectangle - one square at the back and one square at the front. The other end of the **Yellow** rectangle is now sandwiched between two squares. Leave a 1 cm (³/₈″) **GAP** at the start of the sewing.

3 Fold all the **Black** squares away from the two seams to reveal the **Yellow** rectangle. The **Yellow** rectangle now resembles a small bag between the **Black** squares.

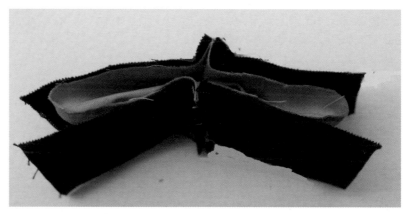

4 Open the top of the **Yellow** rectangle, i.e. open the bag. Bring the two seams together to touch at the centre. The long sides of the **Yellow** rectangle are now folded in half.

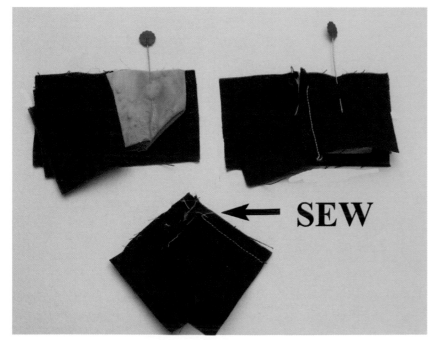

5 Carefully align one of these folded sides of the **Yellow** rectangle with a raw edge of a **Black** square. In addition, match the edge of the opposite **Black** square with the same folded side of the **Yellow** rectangle. (The folded side of the **Yellow** rectangle is now sandwiched between two **Black** squares.) Sew from the centre leaving the same sized **GAP** as before at the start of the stitching.

6 Wiggle everything round and repeat the last stage on the other side so that the last side of the Yellow rectangle is also sandwiched between two **Black** squares. Remember to leave a **GAP** at the start of the sewing!

Don't worry about the gap at the start of each line of stitching. Yes, there will be a small hole at the junction of the seams, but it is hidden at the back of the completed corner square. Without this gap in the stitching the seams of the completed design will not lie flat.

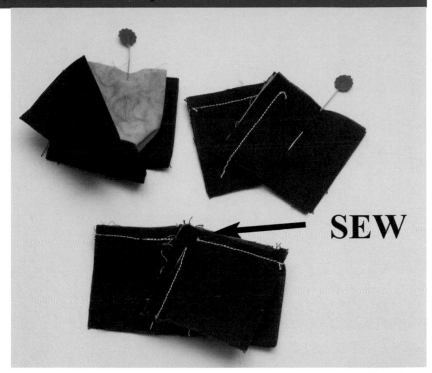

SEW

7 Press all seams open and as flat as possible, put the point of the iron in the centre and spiral the seams in the centre. A good flatten with the iron and a bit of heavy persuasion will ensure that all the seams lie flat.

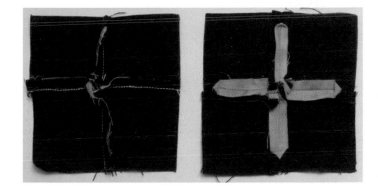

8 Now turn the pressed square over and - magic! There is a **Yellow** square in the middle of four **Black** ones: the **Yellow** square is positioned diagonally (on point) to the outside edges.

9 If you are feeling strong enough, roll back the edges of the **Yellow** centre section and stitch in place.

Alternatively leave well alone as pictured above - it is almost as effective and much less effort!

Once you get the hang of it - these corner squares are simple to make BUT rest assured you can always ignore this design and substitute plain squares of fabric as the corner squares instead.

Attaching Sashing Bands and Corner Squares

This design features nine blocks and requires twenty-four sashing bands and sixteen corner squares. Follow the instructions (page 101), and make all the bands and squares. Some form of incentive might be required to keep your strength up whilst creating all those bands and squares. Beware: chocolate can melt messily all over the material and imbibing wine may make the seams squiffy.

Once you have constructed all those zillions of pieces, attach the relevant sections to the sides of each block in the order shown in the diagram. Use 0.75 cm (¼") S/A. Press all seams open and flat to reduce the bulk.

As each band and block has been accurately measured there should be little need for 'easing', or in layman's jargon - a bit of pulling or pushing of the layers to make them fit.

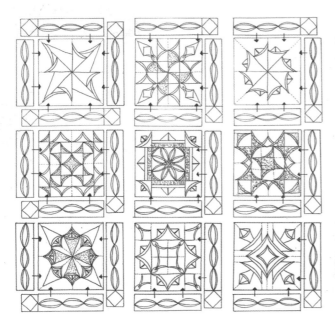

One block has sashing and corners squares added to all four sides, the others have sections sewn to two or three sides only. Constantly checking that the right pieces are on the correct sides is advisable otherwise unpicking may be the order for the day.

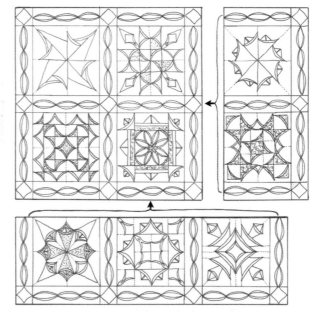

Once all the sashing bands have been added to the relevant sides, join together to make larger sections then sew the larger sections together to complete the panel.

Add the finishing touches with a…
Scalloped Border and a Fan on the corner!

Scalloped Border

21.5 x 123.5 cm **(8½ x 48½″)**
including outer S/A

Cut

Sixty-four 9 cm (3½″) squares - **Black**
Four 8 x 123.5 cm (**3 x 48½″**) strips - **Black**
Thirty-two 9 x 16.5 cm (**3½ x 6½″**) strips - **Orange**
Four 4 x 123.5 cm (**1½ x 48½″**) strips - **Yellow**
Four 5 x 123.5 cm (**2 x 48½″**) strips - **Green**

Start Stitching

Seam allowance 0.75 cm (¼″)

1 Take all sixty-four 9 cm (3½″) **Black** squares plus all thirty-two 9 x 16.5 cm (3½ x 6½″) **Orange** strips and construct thirty-two units as described in Stages 1 - 3, page 95.

2 Join eight units together to make a strip: sew into pairs first, then join two sets of pairs to make a row of four units, i.e. half the strip; repeat with other two sets of pairs, sew both halves to form the strip.

3 Repeat procedure with all other pieces to make three more strips of eight units. Press the seams open and flat.

4 Join one 4 x 123.5 cm (1½ x 48½″) **Yellow** strip to one **Green** one. Press the seam open and flat. Attach this to one side of the **Black** and **Orange** band.

5 Sew one 8 x 123.5 cm (3 x 48½″) **Black** strip to the other side. Stitch both two pieces together with the **Orange** and **Black** strip on the top, then you can see the tip of the inserted **Orange** section in the seam. Sew the seam exactly along the end of the tip. With luck, you will achieve accurate points to the **Orange** triangles on the R/S of the work. Deviating in the seam allowance to accomplish this objective is allowed!

6 Roll back the edges of the Orange triangles and stitch in place. The stitching can be done by hand or machine. For stitch advice - yes, yawn, yawn - go to page 8.

107

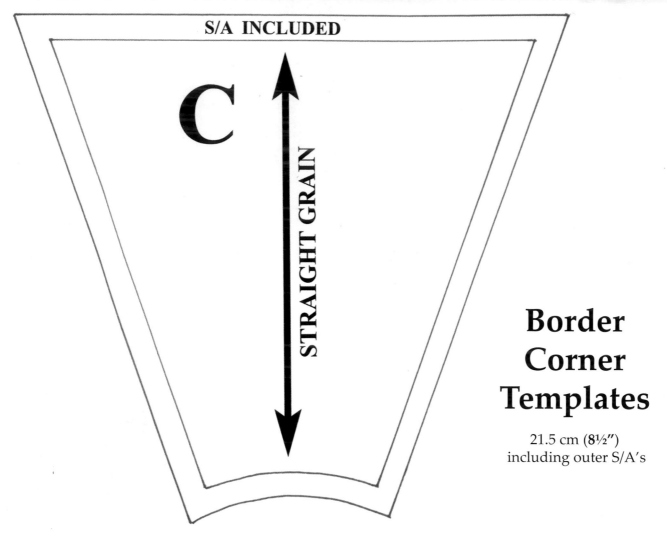

Border Corner Templates

21.5 cm (8½")
including outer S/A's

Trace Templates **C** and **D** on to some form of thin or opaque paper such as greaseproof, baking parchment or tracing paper. Cut the shape out roughly then glue the paper to thin card. Alternatively, trace the template on to template plastic or any transparent material that can be cut with scissors or the rotary cutter. Cut the shape out exactly on the outside line. (If you choose to photocopy as opposed to tracing the template, check the copy in case there are any inaccuracies.)

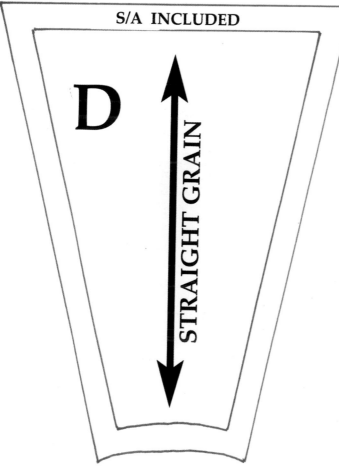

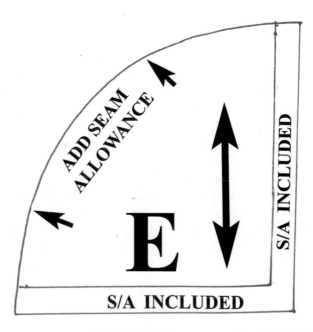

Border Corner

21.5 cm (8½″) including outer S/A

Cut
Four 21.5 cm (8½″) squares - **Black**
Template **C**: Cut Four - **Yellow**
Template **D**: Cut Eight - **Purple**
Four 10 cm (4″) squares - **Green**

Start Stitching
Seam Allowance 0.65 cm (¼″)
(**N.B. Metric S/A is 0.65 cm not 0.75 cm for this pattern**)

1 Following instructions in Stages 1 - 3, page 90, press one **Yellow** shape in half, sew one side, press the seam open and flat then turn R/S out.

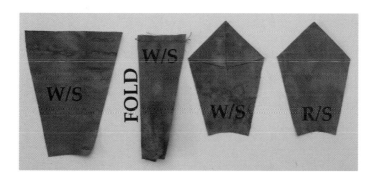

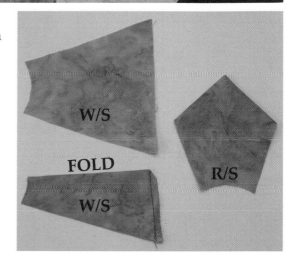

2 Repeat with two **Purple** shapes.

3 Sew the three sections together to form a fan.

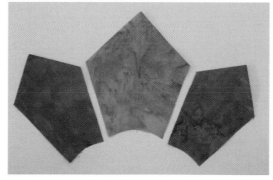

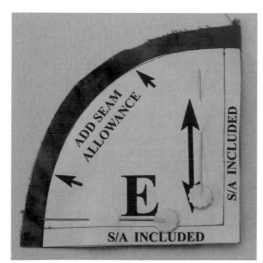

Stitch from the outside edge towards the centre, taking care to line up the edges of the pieces accurately. Press all the seams open and flat.

4 Lay the fan on to a 21.5 cm (8½″) **Black** square R/S up, and pin all the layers carefully together.

5 Trace Template **E** on to thin paper. Lay the paper template on the corner of one 10 cm (4″) **Green** square, lining up the straight sides of template with the raw edges of the **Green** square. Pin in place. Cut the fabric flush with the straight sides of the template but add a generous 0.65 cm (¼″) S/A around the arced edge.

BASTE

ALLOWANCE

S/A INCLUDED

E

S/A INCLUDED

6 Fold the excess fabric over the paper and baste in place. Take care to feed in the little folds accurately.

7 Place on the R/S of the block, lining the straight edges of the template with the raw straight edges of the 21.5 cm (8½″) **Black** square. The edge of this arced shape should cover the raw edges of the fan.

8 Sew round the arc by hand or machine, using one of the stitches (page 8). Remove the basting and the paper should fall out of the sides. Give it a little tug if not.

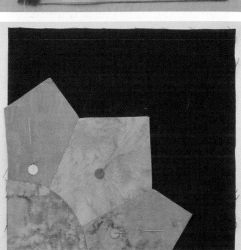

9 Sew round the outer edge; remove all pins and press the block carefully. Baste round both sides of the fan keeping the basting within the S/A.

10 Repeat last stages and make three more blocks.

Adding the Borders

Attach two border strips to the sides of the central panel. Sew the two border corner blocks to both ends of the two remaining border strips and attach to the top and bottom of the quilt.

Yippee - the borders are on, and now you can complete the quilt. Many people have their own ways to finish the quilt but for a very very quick précis...

Just Briefly

There are many sources of information available on completing a quilt i.e. the putting together of three layers (top fabric, wadding/batting, backing fabric) then securing the layers with stitchery or some other means such as a quilting tie. This is just a brief reminder.

Should the completed panel intended as the quilt top need enlarging increase the size by adding more borders. If you are going to embellish the quilt with intricate stitching - one last tip - draw the designs on to the quilt top with a sharp hard pencil before basting the layers together. Press the quilt top well.

Cut some wadding/batting a little larger than the completed quilt top. Lay the backing fabric W/S up on a flat surface. Pin in place or tape the fabric down to keep it wrinkle free. Place the batting/wadding on top and smooth out any creases. Put the quilt top on to the wadding/batting and backing material and smooth out carefully. Pin or tape the quilt top in place.

Working from the centre towards outer edges, pin/baste or use Tak (Tack) gun to anchor all the layers together. Finally baste round the outside edge through all layers - keep the basting within the seam allowance. Trim any excess backing fabric to fit the quilt top.

Machine or hand quilt the layers together. Due to the thick layers of fabric in some seams of the quilt, outline quilting at 0.75 cm (¼") away from seams may be a preferable option to 'stitch in the ditch'. If using the machine try the walking/even-feed foot, or free-motion quilt with the darning/hopper foot. Quilt from the centre outwards. Use a thread colour to coordinate with the fabrics or use invisible thread or nylon filament. Why quilt at all? Try tying the layers together with a quilting tie or simply securing all the layers with a small decorative stitch or button at even intervals.

Finally bind the raw outer edges (see page 86). Label and date your quilt. Hang it up or spread it out and admire.

**Remember nothing is absolutely perfect
but I bet it is pretty good!**

Enjoy twiddling

Jennie Rayment

Glossary

Appliqué Stitch: Small stitch for securing an applied shape or to retain a layer in place.

Backing: The fabric used underneath a sample or the underside of a cushion or quilt.

Baste: Securing of layers with a long stitch to prevent movement.

Batting: See Wadding.

Batik: Hand dyed fabric using a wax resist.

Bias: Diagonal grain-line of the material (45°).

Blind Hem Stitch: Small stitch with 'v' shaped indent which can be used for appliqué.

Calico: UK: Plain woven strong cotton cloth (sometimes bleached), US: floral printed cotton fabric.

Catch: Several small stitches in the same place for securing an edge/corner of material.

Chintz: Close-woven shiny cotton cloth with a resin coating for that characteristic sheen.

Cretonne: Similar to unglazed chintz; see above.

Darning Foot: Used for freehand embroidery and quilting. Used with feed dogs down/covered and stitch width and length settings to zero.

Free Motion Quilting: Securing layers together using lowered feed dogs and darning foot.

Grain: Direction of the weave. Weft fibres run across selvedge to selvedge; warp fibres are parallel to selvedge. Bias grain runs diagonally at 45° to selvedge.

Half Square Triangles: Formed by cutting a square in half diagonally.

Hopper Foot: See Darning foot.

Invisible Thread/Nylon Filament: Robust nylon or similar fibre that is almost colourless - merges with background materials.

Loft: Amount a wadding/batting rises on quilting.

Muslin: UK: Fine soft open weave cotton fabric, in US muslin is the same as the same as UK calico.

Quag: Quilt that folds to form a bag!

Quillow: Quilt forms pillow/cushion when folded

Pinwheel: Rotation of a shape round a central point.

Prairie Points: Squares folded diagonally into quarter triangles.

R/S: Right side of material.

Satin Stitch: The stitched effect produced by increasing stitch width and decreasing length of zigzag pattern.

S/A or Seam Allowance: Distance between the stitch line and the edge of the fabric.

Selvedge/selvage: The firm edges of the fabric running parallel to the warp threads.

Stitch in the Ditch: Following the seam line between pieced shapes.

Somerset/Folded Squares: UK: Squares folded in rectangles then in triangles, US: Sharks Tooth.

Stay Stitching: Securing of layers with a long stitch to prevent movement.

Suffolk Puff: Gathered circle of material.

Tack: UK: Stabilising layers with long stitch, US: small securing stitches in one place.

Tak/Tack Gun: Plastic stapler gun for securing layers

W/S: Wrong or underside of fabric.

Wadding: Batting or filling frequently made from polyester or cotton or wool and silk fibres. Used in between or underneath fabric for quilting purposes.

Index

Appliqué/Blind Hem: 8
Basic Bag: 93
Basting: 8
Bias Strips: 101
Binding a Circle: 17
Blood: Removal on fabric: 46
Border Corner: 109
Borders: 10 - 11, 110, Striped Border: 21
Catherine Wheel: 13, Table Mat: 16,
Catherine Wheel Combination: 23
Corner Square: 103
Criss Cross Stars: 30
Cross Grain: 55
Eight Point Star Cushion: 47
Fabric: choice: 9, washing: 9
Firecracker: 65
Fizgig: 5, Fizgig Whirl: 54
Flying Geese: 97
Girandole: 75
Half Square Triangles: 19
Handles: 56, 94
Invisible Thread/Nylon Filament: 6, 9, 29, 58
Jumping Jack: 25
Mitred Binding: 86
Piping Cushion: 48
Points: Accuracy: 9
Quag: 56
Roman Candle: 69
Sashing: 101, Attaching: 106
Scalloped Border: 107
Scrappy Zappy Do!: 18
Seam Allowance: ¼": 7, 1 cm: 7, ½": 86
Sewing Machine: 6
Skyrocket: 61
Starburst: 81
Stars for Us: 84
Suffolk Puff: 37
Templates: 89, 91,108
Trumpet Cracker: 33, Twiddle: 38, Tote: 39
Twinkling Star: 43
Twirling Pinwheel: 95
Whirlygig: 89

For highly informative, educational and entertaining Workshops and Lectures

Jennie Rayment

5 Queen Street, Emsworth, Hampshire, PO10 7BJ United Kingdom
Tel/Fax: + 44 (0) 1243 374860
e-mail: jenrayment@aol.com

www: jennierayment.com